LEGENDS WORTH LIVING

by
NATHAN DRAZIN

BOOKS BY NATHAN DRAZIN

History of Jewish Education from 515 B.C.E. to 220 C.E.
(English and Hebrew)

Marriage Made in Heaven (English and Hebrew)

Isaac Levinson's Genealogy

LEGENDS WORTH LIVING

by
NATHAN DRAZIN

KTAV PUBLISHING HOUSE, INC.
HOBOKEN, NJ

COPYRIGHT (c) 1991
ISRAEL DRAZIN
Library of Congress Cataloging-in-Publication Data

Drazin, Nathan, 1906-1976
    Legends worth living / by Nathan Drazin
        p.   cm.
    ISBN 0-88125-373-1
    1. Jewish sermons, American.   I. Title.
BM740.2.D73   1991
296.4'2—dc20   90-28181
                                                                      CIP
        Manufactured in the United States of America

Contents

Foreword   ix
Preface   x v

Wit

How to Stop Thirst Without Water	3
A Jew Who Doesn't Observe His Holidays	5
Seven Years of Riches	7
Abraham's Mother	10
A Sermon Out of Nothing	13
No Need to Disturb the Tree	15
Know Your Place	18
The Genuine Moses	20
Dark Sayings of the Wise	24
Words Don't Substitute for Experience	27

Greed

What a Little Silver Can Do	33
He Did Not Have to Pay the Doctor	36
Two Men Who Loved Chicken	38
A Just Demand	41
Beware of Worry	43
Another Tragedy	46
Brass Buttons	48

God's Way

Had Gadya, Had Gadya	53
Man's Limited Mind	56

A Thoughtless Complaint   58
The Wall Answered His Prayer   59
A Dead Monkey Brought Him Gold   62
The Cure for Insomnia   67

Understanding Life
"I'll Never Forgive That Doctor!"   73
King for a Year   74
Where Is Happiness?   77
The Mistake of a Lifetime   80
Distribute Not Thy Wealth in Thy Lifetime   82

Explaining Scriptures
The Truly Great Are Immortal   87
The King Loved Music   90
He Slumbers Not, Nor Sleepeth   92

Marriage
Three Kinds of Wives   97
God Makes Marriages   100
The Doctor's Mistake Made a Man Out of Him   102
The Baal Shem and a Sinner   104
A Pit and a Weasel as Witnesses   107

Foreword

Dad has passed on now, but his story remains. He was a remarkable man.

Nathan Drazin was one of eight children, including an adopted son taken in by his philanthropic parents. Grandfather and grandmother devoted their free time to three pursuits: Torah, worship, and acts of loving-kindness. They established three institutions in Israel: a school wing, a synagogue, and a free loan society.

Dad was born in the United States but spent his early years in Ottawa, the Canadian capital, where his father hired a private teacher of Jewish studies for him and his brothers. While in Ottawa, Dad joined practice to theory. He acquired the skills and rights of a shochet and became a volunteer ritual slaughterer for fowl. While still a teenager he taught an adult Talmud class.

Although offered a lucrative career in his parents' real estate business, Dad—who memorized Malbim's long Hebrew commentary to the Book of Esther at an early age, while devouring books on astronomy and other sciences—chose a scholarly and community service vocation.

He received his M.A. from Columbia College and his Ph.D. from Johns Hopkins University. He was a member of Phi Beta Kappa. His rabbinical degrees, including the prestigious *yadin yadin*, were secured from Yeshiva University.

Dad was just above average height but looked very tall because of his stately figure. He was clean-shaven except for a closely clipped mustache. Always well dressed, he wore

ix

tailored suits and rimless glasses that sharpened his scholarly appearance. His bearing and look both commanded respect, although he never asked for it or seemed to need it. Those of us who observed him closely saw a twinkle in his eyes.

Starting in 1933, he was the rabbi of Shaarei Tfiloh Congregation in Baltimore for thirty-one years, then president of the Talmudical Academy in the same city for five years. He was president during the period that this Jewish day school reached its zenith in number of students and in quality of its education. He was responsible for building its expansive and impressive campus. His final position, upon emigrating to Israel, was as director of the Institute for Judaism and Medicine. In this capacity, in which he served for seven years, he edited a Hebrew manual for physicians on ethical questions.

Dad's accomplishments during his forty-three years of community service are well-known. Among other things, he helped found the Ner Israel Rabbinical College, served as the head of its education committee for years, and taught homiletics to its graduate students. Although he achieved rabbinic prominence and improved the Baltimore day schools, Dad refused high-paying positions elsewhere—including that of Chief Rabbi of South Africa and professor in one of its universities—because he felt that Baltimore had the best Jewish schools for his children anywhere outside of New York. With his book *Marriage Made in Heaven*, he brought the subject of sex into the open even in the most pious homes. He started the group that still oversees kosher laws in Maryland and secured civil legal authority for the enterprise. He was always zionistically inclined and was the president of the Seaboard Region of Mizrachi. It was he who suggested to the Israeli government that it persuade rabbis to appeal for Israeli bonds during the High Holy Days, when Jewish sentiments are high. His suggestion, known as the Baltimore Plan, was accepted worldwide and resulted in many millions of dollars for Israel that would never have been collected otherwise.

Dad was a Renaissance man, who, in a Maimonidean fash-

ion, had broad intellectual and cultural interests encompass-
ing the full spectrum of available knowledge. The books in his
home library, in several languages, three walls side to side
and top to bottom, reflected his interests: Bible and Talmud
classics faced the ancient works of Greece and Rome, England, Russia, France, and others. There were volumes on
psychology, philosophy, mysticism, history, education, astronomy, medicine, and sex. He was a scrupulously observant
Orthodox Jew who sat and studied the Talmud in his library
at least several hours every day, in an atmosphere of silent
piety sometimes punctuated by the traditional chant used by
Talmud scholars who vocalize the text. He spent hours daily
studying with another rabbi. His desk was surrounded by
more than a sprinkling of books by religious scoffers, modern-
ists, biblical critics, and even two versions of the New Testament in two different Hebrew translations. Upon settling in
the holy city of Jerusalem, he expanded the scope of his
studies to include the Jerusalem Talmud, a text rarely studied
by rabbinic scholars. Recognizing that a sound mind requires
a sound body, he combined his daily exercising of his mind
with a half-hour session of physical exercise each day. He
enjoyed exercising with his grandchildren, and could be seen
with them early in the morning stretched out on the floor.

Dad wrote hundreds of scholarly articles in English, Hebrew, and Yiddish, and several books. He edited several
others, including a Talmud commentary and the above-men-
tioned ethical guide. He was a brilliant speaker. He had a
remarkable ability to focus on the point at issue and articulate
it clearly. And he loved to tell stories, and did it well. Looking
back, I realize that it was a device used by this agile-minded
scholar to make points that we, with lesser minds, could not
otherwise understand.

He could grip one with his stories and hold their attention.
We listened because of the plots and the way he told them.
We realized that they were guiding lights, illuminating the
creases and crevices of life's hazardous road.

Dad died a month after his seventieth birthday from an incurable cancer that he knew was terminal. He was careful at the end not to place any burden on anyone. He rose from his sick-bed to put his affairs in order.

It is not surprising that the story of Dad's life is remembered and retold. And it is a proper tribute to his memory that the stories he compiled before his death should be published now, fourteen years later, in honor of Mom's birthday.

* * *

Mom too is a Renaissance person. Unlike most women of her age, she had an extensive Judaic education, attended a teachers training school, and secured a diploma in teaching. Her siblings included community leaders and educators, the world-renowned biblical scholar and historian Sidney B. Hoenig, and the well-known lawyer Moses H. Hoenig, an organizer of Young Israel of America. During the depression, while her brothers and sisters attended school, she added financial support to her family. She taught in a New York City public school daily from 9:00 a.m. to 3:00 p.m. and 4:00 p.m. to 7:00 p.m., at the English Department of Yeshiva Torah Vodaath, including Sundays. She helped the youngsters in her public school classes learn to read Hebrew by having the neighborhood synagogue open its doors for her during the evenings after 8:00 p.m. Mom charged 10 cents a lesson, feeling, correctly, that it would give the children an incentive to learn. She returned the money to them in the form of Purim and Chanukah gifts.

Due to financial difficulties caused by the depression, Yeshiva Torah Vodaath never paid Mom six months of her $60 a month salary. With interest, this debt of fifty-seven years would be quite a sum.

Mom's dad, my grandfather Joseph Isaac Hoenig, also donated free services to the Yeshiva, as a leading member of its board of directors. The Yeshiva noted his service by giving Mom a set of silver candlesticks as a wedding gift. She gave them years later to my wife Dina, who lights them on Sabbath eve.

Mom's dad died when I was only six weeks old, so I do not remember him, but I remember his wife, Mom's mom, my grandmother. She had a marvelous sense of humor, and, apropos this book, she was an articulate raconteur.

Mom left teaching to marry Dad in 1933. She has an alert and practical mind, and still reads several books a week. She advised me well when she suggested that I pursue a secular career in addition to Judaic studies.

Although eighty two years old today, Mom stands erect, dresses well, and looks young for her age, like the oldest person in Dad's tale "Three Kinds of Wives." Dad liked this story a lot, not because it was the best, but because it reflected his relationship with Mom.

ISRAEL DRAZIN

Preface

When God gave the Ten Commandments on Mount Sinai, according to a Talmudic legend, donkeys did not bray, dogs did nor growl, horses did not neigh, and birds did not chirp. Perfect quiet prevailed on earth.

Silence was granted then for man so that his concentration might be undisturbed and his comprehension of the lofty truths be unimpaired.

Allegories and legends can also help man's perception and understanding. When the wisest of men taught people knowledge, "he pondered, and sought out, and set in order many proverbs" (Ecclesiastes 12:9). The Hebrew word for "proverbs," *meshalim*, denotes allegories, aphorisms, and legends.

The legends in this volume were selected because of their general interest, with the hope that they may serve as sources of illumination to those who search for the good and desirable in life. The brief comments that follow each legend attempt to illustrate such values with at least one example.

The legends were collected from various sources over a period of many years. Some the author heard orally; others he gathered from old books published in various countries; a few appeared in brief form in Israeli newspapers. Some contemporary stories, which by their nature will in time surely become legends, were also included. All were edited and embellished for this publication.

In Israel today there is a *kibbutz galuyot*, an ingathering of exiles, communities of Jews from the different countries of the world, each with its own language, its own customs, and its own legends, yet all one people. The author desired to dramatize this fact by giving the original locality of each legend to the best of his knowledge.

The author gratefully acknowledges his indebtedness to his son Rabbi Israel Drazin, of Columbia, Maryland, for his helpful suggestions in the preparation of this volume. To his wife, Celia H. Drazin, the author acknowledges a deep debt of gratitude for her gentle encouragement at all times—a true "helpmeet."

March 1974   N.D.

How to Stop Thirst Without Water

Yom Kippur, the Day of Atonement, is a very strict Jewish fast-day. It is biblically ordained: "Ye shall afflict your souls . . . from evening unto evening" (Leviticus 23:32). Thus Jews abstain from food and drink for more than twenty-four hours, from before sundown until after sundown of the following day.

Once, in the large synagogue of Sandez, Galicia, on a *Yom Kippur* afternoon, a certain Jew felt very faint. Those sitting beside him made light of it. "It serves him right," they whispered, "let him feel what it means to go thirsty and hungry." Their victim was none other than Berel, "the Rich Miser." He was one of the richest men in the city, but had been given this nickname because of his notorious miserliness.

After a few moments, however, when his neighbors noticed that Berel had become dangerously pale, they knew that this was a serious matter. They called over the dayan, who served as the assistant rabbi, to tell them what to do. He advised that they serve Berel a few drops of water on a teaspoon. This did not help the miser, who murmured feebly: "I need a full glass of water or I will die!"

The dayan, frightened by the words, rushed to the rabbi of the synagogue and community, Rabbi Chayim Halberstam, for advice. On hearing who was involved, the rabbi responded: "Tell Berel that he may drink as many glasses of water as he needs, *but* for every glass of water that he drinks, he must pledge one hundred gulden for the synagogue."

3

When the miser heard the rabbi's decision, a tremendous change swept over him. He sat up erect and did not feel faint any longer. He did not need any water. He was not thirsty at all.

COMMENT

Where did the rabbi obtain the psychological insight that enabled him to deal with the miser's extreme thirst?

In the Jerusalem Talmud we find the following declaration: "All the limbs of man are attached to the heart, and the heart is tied to the pocketbook."

Physicians would approve the first half of this statement. But how do we understand the second half?

Rabbi Chayim Halberstam (1793–1876), popularly known as Reb Chayim Sandzer, was held in the highest esteem by the learned rabbis of his generation for his sincere piety and profound scholarship. He understood its meaning. There is a *psychological* tie-up between a man's heart and his pocketbook.

A Jew Who Doesn't Observe
His Holidays

Motka Chabad was famous for his wit. He lived several generations too soon. In his day there was no radio or television. He had no opportunity to become a popular star and wealthy. Thus, despite his wit, he was poor. In fact, years of poverty affected his growth. He was emaciated and short. His only asset was his wit. That never failed him.

One day, as he was walking along the streets of Vilna, absorbed in thought, he accidentally bumped into a Russian peasant. Motka immediately apologized, but the peasant was enraged. He lifted his hand and slapped Motka across the face. Motka looked up at his opponent, a huge, heavy-set, giant of a man—little Motka was no match from him. Revenge is sweet. But how? Fortunately his wit did not fail him. He put his hand into his pocket, took out two *kopecks*, and offered them to his adversary.

"Why are you giving me money?" the peasant asked.

"Don't you know? Haven't you heard? We Jews have a special holiday today. If someone slaps us today, we must put our hand in our pocket and give whatever money we find to the one who struck us. It so happens," Motka continued, "that I'm a very poor Jew. All I had in my pocket were the *kopecks* I gave you. But do you see that house?" Motka was pointing a finger at a large house. "There lives the richest Jew in town. If you knock on his door and slap him as you did me, he will put his hand in his pocket, and who knows? He may give you one hundred rubles."

5

Now, the peasant had never seen one hundred rubles at one time. So with great enthusiasm and visions of riches, without a word of thanks, he ran to the house and banged on the door. As fortune would have it, the rich Jew himself opened the door. Without a word the peasant smacked him hard across the face. The Jew screamed and servants ran to his rescue. They grabbed the peasant, held him, and beat him. Never before had he received such a beating. When they were satisfied that he would never raise his hand against their employer again, they threw him into the gutter. There, lying in the filth, writhing in pain, hardly able to rise, the peasant, glancing toward Motka Chabad, was overheard mumbling, "The nerve of that little Jew! To send me to a Jew who doesn't observe his holidays!"

COMMENT

Motka Chabad may be said to represent the Jewish people in exile. Without their homeland, for almost two thousand years, Jews were the constant butt of bullies and anti-Semites. That they were able to survive may be attributed, at least in part, to the development of their wit.

They were unlike the navigators in Psalms 107:27 who "reeled to and fro, and staggered like a drunken man, and all their wit was swallowed up."

"Look," wrote William Shakespeare (1564–1616) *The Tempest* II, 1, 12, "he's winding up the watch of his wit; by and by it will strike."

Seven Years of Riches

There was a poor but pious man who lived in Babylon with his wife and five young children. He went looking for work every morning and brought his earnings home every evening. What he earned was generally insufficient to feed his family.

One morning he looked for work as usual, but none could be found. He searched unsuccessfully the entire day. That evening he returned with nothing. There was no food, and his wife put their children to sleep hungry. The next morning, when they awoke, they were all crying for food. When their mother saw their tears and knew that she could not help them, she too wept. The father restrained his own tears with difficulty. He put on his coat and left the house, praying: "O God, give us bread for the sake of our innocent children."

As soon as the father reached the street he was approached by a stranger who appeared to be an elderly rabbi. The stranger had a pleasing countenance and a long flowing white beard. He said to the father: "Friend, you will have seven years of riches. Tell me. Do you want them now or at the end of your life?"

This was an unusual question. The man was mystified, but he replied: "Rabbi, I have a partner in life—my wife. Give me time to consult with her, and then I'll give you our choice."

Permission was granted. When the wife heard the question she was also mystified, but only for a brief moment. Feeling the hunger of their young children, she answered: "Tell the rabbi that we want the seven years of riches *now*."

When the bearded stranger heard the reply, he said: "Go back to your house. Dig in the southeastern corner of your cellar. You will find a metal box there, full of gold coins. They are yours, for seven years."

The father rushed home, and, as promised, within a few moments, his family became one of the richest in the land.

The family never forgot its poverty. Every day they sought to do good deeds. They visited schoolhouses. When they found children barefooted, they would buy them shoes. When they saw children in tatters, they would buy them new clothes. They fed the undernourished. They did their best to satisfy the needs of the poor.

Time passed all too quickly. One morning when the man left his home, he saw the stranger waiting for him. "The seven years are up," he said. "I have come to take back the riches that I gave you."

The man was surprised and frightened. Had the seven years really ended? What could he say? Then, as an intuition, based more on habit than on thought, he reminded the stranger: "You remember that seven years ago I told you I had a partner in life with whom I would like to consult. Let me consult with my wife again. After I talk to her, I will give you your answer."

Permission was granted. When the wife heard that the rabbi had returned to take away the riches he had given them, she, too, was surprised and frightened. It was hard to believe that seven years had passed. They had flown by so quickly. But such is life.

"This is no ordinary rabbi," the woman said to her husband. "He must be an angel disguised as a rabbi. What can we say to such a person? The riches were a gift for seven years. We enjoyed it and should be thankful, and we must accept that the time is up." Then she added: "All that we can say is this. If God, in His wisdom, knows people who are worthier custodians of His money, then by all means let Him take it and turn it over to those better people. But if God has found us worthy keepers of His money, then let Him leave it with us awhile longer. We will continue to practice the acts of loving-kindness that we believe He likes us to do.''

When the man returned with this answer, he found the stranger smiling: "God heard your virtuous wife's reply. He has not found better custodians of His money. You may keep the riches as long as you continue your daily acts of charity, even as long as you live.''

COMMENT

This legend depicts the ethical teaching of Rabbi Eleazar in the Ethics of the Fathers: "Give Him of what is His, for you and what you have are His" (3:8).

Genesis 2:16 "You may eat of every tree of the garden except from the tree of good and evil" informs us that everything belongs to God. We steal from God when we take anything from anyone.

All that man has—life, health, wealth—are really gifts to man from a kind Providence. All that God asks as return payment is that we live a virtuous life, "to act justly, to love mercy, and to walk humbly with thy God" (Micah 6:8).

Abraham's Mother

Baghdad, Iraq's capital, is identified by some as the ancient biblical city of Ur Kasdim, where Abraham, the father of the Jewish people, was born. Many of the people of Baghdad took pride in this belief and pointed it out to their visitors.

Once, on a cold winter day, snow fell in Baghdad, a rare occurrence. The sultan, the ruler of the land, suggested to his vizier, a high official, that he ride with him through the streets to see how the people were behaving in the unusual weather. The vizier laughed. He was sure that no one would be outside.

The sultan insisted, however. They wrapped themselves in warm clothing, took a heated chariot, and drove through Baghdad.

The streets were deserted, as the vizier had expected. The people had secluded themselves, bundled warm, in their homes, hidden from the unexpected and somewhat frightening cold. The sultan and the vizier saw only one man walking along the streets. They overtook him, stopped the chariot, summoned the man, and urged him to join them in the coach. It was a Jew, Isaac Haben, on his way to the synagogue for the evening services.

Seeing that the stranger was a Jew, and anticipating a little fun, the sultan took a bundle of money from his pocket and divided it into two equal parts. Putting one part in his pocket and holding the other high, he turned to Isaac. "I will ask you a question," he said. "If you give me the correct answer, this money is yours."

Isaac Haben accepted the challenge. He had nothing to lose!

10

"Tell me," said the sultan, "who was the mother of the father of your people, Abraham?"

This was a difficult question. Abraham's mother is not mentioned in the Bible. Only his father's name, Terah, is recorded. The Talmud mentions the mother's name in one place. The sultan was certain that the Jew would not know the answer.

Isaac Haben, however, was a regular synagogue worshipper. He attended the Talmud class that was taught after the evening service. That year the class was studying tractate Baba Batra of the Babylonian Talmud, where Abraham's mother's name is mentioned. He responded immediately.

"Abraham's mother's name was Amtalai, daughter of Karnvo," he answered.

The sultan handed the money to Isaac. "You won it fairly," he said.

Isaac Haben turned to the sultan with his own proposal. "Your Honor, if I may, I'd like to ask you a question. If you know the answer, I will give you back the money. But if you do not know the answer, you will give me the other half that you put in your pocket."

The sultan liked the challenge. It was an excellent way to pass the winter day. He nodded assent: "Go ahead, ask your question."

"Your Honor," said Isaac Haben, "you asked me the name of a woman who died more than four thousand years ago; I'll ask you the name of a woman who died here, in this city, only four months ago. What was the name of my mother?"

The sultan laughed and he turned over the remaining money to Isaac. "You are a wise, wise man," he exclaimed. "You win."

COMMENT

For Jews, Torah learning and wisdom were synonymous. Mothers would put their babes to sleep with a Yiddish lullaby: *Torah iz die beste sechorah*, "Torah is the best merchandise."

King Solomon stated: "Happy is the man that findeth wisdom. . . . She is more precious than rubies, and all the things thou canst desire are not to be compared unto her. Length of days is in her right hand; in her left hand are riches and honor." (Proverbs 3:13–18).

A Sermon Out of Nothing

The old rabbi of Rothenburg in Bavaria passed away. The seven city officials began to look for a replacement. They heard of young Rabbi Meir ben Baruch (later known as Maharam m'Rothenburg), and invited him to speak to their community during a Sabbath service.

Before a new rabbi was elected in Rothenburg in the thirteenth century, the seven officials would decide on a topic for the candidate to preach on in his trial sermon. The topic was written on a sheet of paper and put in an envelope. As the rabbi stood on the pulpit on Sabbath morning, the sexton would bring him the envelope. The candidate, of course, had not seen the paper before. If he was able to speak extemporaneously on the topic and inspire the people, he would have a good chance of becoming the rabbi of Rothenburg.

In accordance with the custom, the seven officials met in secret and selected a biblical passage, wrote it on a sheet of paper, placed it in an envelope, and hid it in a secret place in the synagogue, there to wait until the last moment when Rabbi Meir ben Baruch was standing on the pulpit.

When Rabbi Meir arrived in town, even before he spoke, a strong opposition arose to his candidacy. The former rabbi had been a man with personality. He had been tall, erect, with a long flowing beard. His demeanor commanded respect. Rabbi Meir, on the other hand, was short and young, his beard had hardly sprouted, and what was worse, he was slightly hunchbacked. His physical appearance caused part of the community to decide against him. However, all agreed not to shame him and to let him speak at the Sabbath service.

We all know that every rule has its exception. One man decided that the rabbi should not speak. He knew the envelope's hiding place. Unknown to all, he removed the sheet and substituted a blank sheet of paper. "Now the rabbi will have nothing to say," the sneak muttered.

The synagogue was packed that Sabbath morning. Rabbi Meir walked to the pulpit, and the sexton came forward with the envelope. The rabbi removed the sheet and unfolded it. It was blank. He turned it over. It was blank on the other side as well. The people watched his every move. They were upset by what they saw. Who could have done this, to disgrace a man in public? Rabbi Meir retained his calm. With only a brief moment of reflection, he held the blank sheet of paper high so that all could see it. He exclaimed in Judeo-German, *Ya, Raboti, von garnichts hat Gott die Welt baschafen!* ("Yes, my friends, out of nothing did God create the world!")

Then, using this exclamation as his text, he delivered a sermon with learning and humor that left the congregation spellbound. The people sensed the intelligence and noble character of the rabbi who stood before them. All opposition melted away. The next day Rabbi Meir was elected the rabbi of Rothenburg, unanimously.

COMMENT

A woman said to her rabbi: "I love your sermons. You get so much from your text that isn't really there."

"It is not sufficient to know what one ought to say, but one must also know how to say it" Aristotle (384–322 B.C.E.) *Rhetoric,* Book 3, chapter 1.

"An ounce of mother-wit is worth a pound of clergy" Andrew Marvell (1621–78) *Growth of Poetry.*

No Need to Disturb the Tree

A Jewish jeweler from Marrakesh traveled for several months each year through various cities of his country to sell his merchandise. He returned home only after he sold his goods.

One Friday afternoon, he sold his merchandise but had no time to return before the Sabbath. Fortunately, he was in Meknès, where he had an acquaintance. He visited this person and asked if he could be accommodated for the Sabbath. He was welcomed. Later, before the Sabbath, he gave his purse filled with cash to his host for safekeeping over the weekend.

On Sunday morning, when the jeweler was ready to leave, he asked his host for his purse.

"What purse!" said his host. "You never gave me a purse!" He denied all knowledge of the money.

The jeweler was frightened. He saw himself impoverished. But perhaps his host had only forgotten. He tried to remind him of the circumstances surrounding his handing him the purse. He pleaded with his host to return the money to him. It was all in vain. His host became angry. "How dare you accuse me of thievery!" he shouted.

The jeweler, seeing that this man, his erstwhile friend, meant to rob him of his savings, went to the sage, Rabbi Hayim ben Moses ibn Atar (1696–1743), and asked that his host be summoned for trial. The request was granted. When the rabbi heard the jeweler's complaint, he turned to the defendant and said: "What do you say about this charge?"

15

"He is lying. He never gave me a purse," was the brazen reply.

"Did anyone see you handing this man your purse?" the rabbi asked, turning to the plaintiff.

The stranger thought for a moment and then replied: "I cannot say that anyone saw me handing him the purse, but I remember that when I handed it to him we were standing in the shade of one of the many palm trees that surround his estate."

"Good! Wonderful!" the rabbi remarked jubilantly. "Go tell the tree that I summon it to come here to testify. The tree will be the witness in this case!"

Rabbi Hayim was famous not only for his learning and piety but also for his knowledge of *Kabbalah,* mysticism, and wondrous doings. Without question or hesitation, therefore, the jeweler left to do as he was told.

The rabbi and the defendant remained in the house. The rabbi paced the floor, walking slowly from one end of the room to the other. He mumbled words quietly, under his breath. After two minutes, his words were audible: "The man is now at the tree ready to talk to it."

"Not yet," the man burst out, not thinking.

"You thief, you stole the purse," the rabbi thundered. "How would you know where the tree is if you had never received the purse? You will return the purse with all its contents or you will be severely punished!" The thief had no choice but to obey.

The rabbi's admiring followers sang his praises for years afterwards: "How great and wonderful our rabbi is! He was able to decide the case without even disturbing the tree!"

COMMENT

A judge needs more than technical legal knowledge to decide a case. Wit is an invaluable addition to his mental equipment.

This is why when King Solomon was given the choice, he responded: "Give Thy servant an understanding heart to judge Thy people, that I may discern between good and evil" (I Kings 3:9).

Know Your Place

Rabbi Moses Isaac of Chelm (1828–1900), known as the Chelmer Maggid, was a popular itinerant preacher for half a century. He preached in virtually every Polish city and town. People flocked to hear the parables and legends with which he would spice his discourses.

This was one of the preacher's favorites.

A wealthy man married off his daughter—an only child—and his joy was overflowing. Eager to share his happiness with his townsfolk, he invited them to the wedding and to the grand feast that followed. To make sure that all his guests would enjoy themselves no matter what their social background, he had his chef prepare three menues, so that everyone would be served the kind of meal he was accustomed to. The rich were given hors d'oeuvres, stuffed nesting pigeons, and expensive liquors. The tables of the middle class were set with hot gefilte fish, sliced turkey, and sweet wine. The poor had large plates heaped with chopped herring, sliced herring, hot potatoes, black bread, and beer. "All my guests will remember my daughter's feast with joy, all their lives," the happy wealthy man said contentedly.

One of his guests was a *nouveau riche*, one who had come into money only recently. His seat was among the rich, but when he tasted the hors d'oeurvres, they were unfamiliar to him, and he could not develop an appetite for them. He nibbled on the pigeon, but without relish. Even the liquors were not agreeable to his taste. His mouth watered when he looked at the tables of the poor, laden with the kinds of food

18

and drink that he was accustomed to, a meal that he knew he would enjoy. Unable to withstand temptation, he rose from his seat and rushed to the table of the poor. He returned to his seat with a plate full of herring, hot potatoes, and black bread and a large mug of beer. Unexpectedly, however, the food affected him badly. The beer did not mix with the liquors he had imbibed. He felt that the large hall, the tables, and the people were whirling about him; he was dizzy and unsteady; his head and hands fell to the table, crashing several dishes to the floor.

When the host rushed over to see what was wrong, he found his guest leaning helplessly on the table with remnants of herring, potatoes, and beer splashed near him. Instinctively he realized what had happened. He had the waiters carry the guest to a cot in the rear of the room where he could lie comfortably until he was sober.

To the other guests, who were asking what had happened, the host replied: "One man did not know his place; the poor fellow could not decide where he belonged."

COMMENT

The Chelmer Maggid used his legend to dramatize a number of ethical precepts. If a man would only remember his place, his origin as well as his latter end, he would not fall into the trap of foolish pride and arrogance. He would also be saved from sinful passions and the lust for money.

"For the world was built in order
And the atoms march in tune."

Ralph Waldo Emerson
(1803–1882)
Monadnock

The Genuine Moses

The rule of the Yemenite sultans, beginning in the dark twelfth century, when civilization seemed to slumber, brought persecution and misery to the Jewish inhabitants.

This was especially true during the reign of Sultan Ahmed, whose name means "love." How he acquired this incongruous name is a mystery, but the sultan's parents, like most people, were probably ignorant of the significance of the names they give their children.

Sultan Ahmed had a Vizier whose name was Haman. Like his biblical namesake, he was a vicious anti-Semite. Everyday Vizier Haman seemed to devise some new way to humiliate the Jews.

One day, he came to the sultan with an ingenious idea.

"The Jews claim that their religion and all their laws were handed to them by a prophet named Moses who lived more than two thousand years ago. But how is this possible? This man has been dead for two thousand years, and yet they observe his rules as if he were alive and watching them.

"I believe that he must still be alive. I'm sure that if you order the Jews to do so, they will bring him to you. It would be quite interesting to meet this man, and great sport."

The sultan was pleased with this proposal and, having nothing better to do, ordered that the seven leading Jews of the community be rushed to his palace.

When they arrived, the sultan told them: "I know that your prophet Moses is still alive and in hiding. There is no use trying to fool me further. Bring him here within a week. If you don't, I'll drive all of you Jews out of my land without your possessions. This is just, and my final word!''

When the frightened Jews tried to explain that what he was asking was impossible, that Moses was indeed dead and had been so for two thousand years, the sultan laughed at them and ordered them to leave.

The news of the devilish decree fell like an unwelcome thunderbolt upon the Jewish community, frightening everyone. A three-day fast was ordained by the rabbis, in the tradition of the fast ordered by Queen Esther and Mordecai in the earlier days of the biblical Haman, to plead with God to repeat His performance of a miraculous delivery. The three days were spent in the synagogues by men, women, and children, devoted to pious prayers, copious tears, and scrupulous fasting, but with little hope of success.

On the third day, when all were weakened by their devout activities, an inspired elderly Jew walked over to the rabbis and volunteered to go to the sultan disguised as Moses.

"You have nothing to lose," he explained. With God's help, I'll convince them that I am Moses. If I fail, they will kill only me for this pretense, but the rest of you will probably be spared.''

With no other suggestion or inspiration, the community leaders accepted the old man's idea. They spent the next few days devising ways to impress the sultan with the man's age. They lined his face with deep wrinkles, painted his hair white, and marked his face and hands with huge liver spots appropriate for a man who had survived centuries. On the seventh day, the women clothed him in a white silk caftan like the one they imagined the real Moses must have worn, and handed him an impressive stick that resembled their mental picture of Moses' staff.

So garbed, the old man made an imposing figure. On the seventh day, the Jewish leaders presented him to the sultan and vizier, with an elaborate respectful ceremony befitting the ancient prophet.

"Here, Your Highness," the seven leaders declared, as they bowed low before the man called "love," trying to hide their fear and to distance themselves from the deception, "this man will tell you that he is Moses."

"Is this all?" the vizier smiled roguishly. "Is this enough?" Do you really believe that the sultan will accept this man at your word? We would like to see him perform some miracles as he did in ancient days, to be sure that he really is your prophet."

The old man responded in a practiced, appropriate voice, cracked and hoarse with age: "I will be happy to perform a miracle for you, just as you ask. One miracle should suffice. If you desire it, fine, you shall see and enjoy it. If not, then so be it. I cannot tarry here. I must return to my seclusion.

"Here is the miracle. Listen well. Take a large metal tub, one that can retain heat, and fill it with boiling water. Throw three red-hot bricks into the tub. That will make it really scolding. Then take the honorable vizier and lower him gently, respectfully, but naked, into the tub, and cover all of him with the boiling water for twenty minutes. Then I'll perform the miracle. I'll cause him to rise, alive, looking younger by twenty years. Now surely this is the miracle that you are looking for, a miracle that no one else can perform."

When the vizier saw his master listening intently, seemingly delighted at the sport, he was frightened that the sultan would be persuaded to accept the test at his expense. He could feel himself being boiled alive. So, before the sultan could react, he jumped up and cried aloud: "You have persuaded us. This is the genuine Moses. No need for any test. This is the genuine Moses. No doubt about it."

COMMENT

In about the second century, Quintus Curtius Rufus wrote in *De Rebus Gestis Alexandri Magni* (4:3:22): "Fear makes men ready to believe the worst.'' In this story it made a man believe the best.

God protects His people through mysterious and sometimes humorous ways.

Dark Sayings of the Wise

In the early nineteenth century a poor Jew left his home, his wife, and his family to seek his fortune in a new country. He arrived in Caracas, the capital of Venezuela, and settled there. He started a business, worked hard, and was quite successful.

The man set a definite goal for himself. As soon as he was able to save one hundred thousand dollars, he would return home to Morocco and live with his family in comfort. He outlined his plan in a letter to his wife and expressed confidence that he would achieve his goal in three to five years at the most.

The man was industrious and wise and achieved his aim in record time. However, something unforeseen happened. As he was getting ready to leave for home, he became gravely ill and was rushed to a hospital. He felt his end approaching and was certain that the doctors would be unable to restore him to health.

He called two of his friends to his bedside. Both were fellow Jews who also hailed from Morocco. One had plans to return to Morocco within a few days. The other was a member of the Jewish burial society in Caracas and was planning to visit Morocco several weeks later.

He gave the latter sufficient money for the expenses that might be incurred at the hospital and for his eventual burial. To the first he handed a bundle of money, saying haltingly: "Here is one hundred thousand dollars. You're going to Morocco. Please give my wife what you want. The rest is yours." As he finished the sentence, he breathed his last breath. He was dead.

When the messenger arrived in Morocco he visited his deceased friend's wife, telling her the sad news about her husband and his last request. "He left the division of his money up to me," he continued. "He specifically said, 'Please give my wife what you want. The rest is yours.' Here is what I want to give you." Saying this he put ten thousand dollars on the table, turned, and departed.

The woman was heartbroken. She grieved for her husband, faithfully observing the traditional seven days of intense mourning at her home.

When the seven days concluded, she thought of the messenger's words. They were incomprehensible. She could hardly believe that her husband, whom she had loved dearly, would want to divide his estate in such an unusual and heartless manner.

She went to the rabbinical court of her city and had the messenger summoned for trial. A date was set for the hearing, and both parties were ordered to deposit all the money from the deceased's estate with the court until the final decision was rendered. At the same time both parties were advised to be sure to bring any pertinent evidence they might have to court on the day that the case was heard.

Both parties prepared themselves for the trial. The messenger found that the other friend of the deceased, who was present when the last bequest was made, had arrived in the meantime in Morocco. He summoned him as a witness. The wife, on the other hand, collected all the letters she had received from her husband in the last few years. These clearly conveyed his love and concern for her and the children, and spoke explicitly of his hope to have one hundred thousand dollars for the family on which they could live comfortably for many years.

When the trial date arrived, all the evidence was presented to the court. The messenger and his friend testified that these were the last words of the deceased: "Give my wife what you want. The rest is yours." The voluminous correspondence that the wife presented to the court showed that the deceased was a loving husband who had never dreamed of giving the bulk of his estate to anyone but his family.

After scrutinizing the evidence for several hours, the court gave its final decision: "We find that the deceased in the last moments of his life did say to the messenger, 'Give my wife what you want.' But what did he mean by these words? In reviewing all the evidence we see that this man was prudent and wise. He wanted to be sure that his money would not be stolen or hidden from his wife. He therefore said, 'Give my wife what you want,' meaning, 'what you want; that is, want for yourself.' Now this man wants ninety thousand dollars for himself. We therefore order that ninety thousand dollars be turned over to the wife, and the remaining ten thousand dollars be given to the messenger."

COMMENT

King Solomon, in the introductory verses to his Book of Proverbs, explains the aim of the proverbs as follows: "To know wisdom and instruction, to comprehend the words of understanding; to receive the discipline of wisdom, justice and right and equity . . . to understand a proverb and the interpretation, the words of the wise and their dark sayings" (Proverbs 1:2–6). This legend illustrates how and why a "dark saying" of the wise was employed, and how in the end it was correctly illuminated.

Words Don't Substitute for Experience

When Frederick the Great, the soldier-emperor of Prussia, was carrying out his campaign of conquest, his army surrounded a well-fortified city. Frederick was confident that the inhabitants would be starved into surrender within a short time.

Weeks passed, however, and there was no surrender. Frederick realized that there might be an underground tunnel through which the townspeople were importing their food. Daring as he was, he decided to verify this himself. He disguised himself as a poor civilian, and early one morning, before daybreak, he crept into the city. He walked the streets seemingly unconcerned with any problem, as one would walk toward his home. But he chose the streets adjoining the fortification walls to spy them out. Two hours after he entered the city, when the sun had fully risen, he came upon the object of his hunt. Here was the exit of the hidden tunnel. Weary horses were trudging out of the tunnel with wagons loaded with food. Frederick noted the location and began to think of a way to escape from the city unnoticed.

Suddenly, to his surprise, he heard someone screaming out, "Frederick! It's Frederick the Great!"

He had been recognized! His life was at stake. With a crowd of townspeople in pursuit, he ran into a side street, then into another, then another, and still another. It seemed as if he had evaded the pursuers. He knew, however, that they would search the entire city, and that an organized search,

27

beginning in minutes, would lead to his capture. How could
he escape?

Nearby he noticed the shop of a poor Jewish cobbler. He
entered the shop and said to the cobbler: "Listen, I am
Frederick the Great. People know I am in town and the army
will be looking for me. If you hide me and save my life, I will
grant you three requests."

The offer was tempting, hard to refuse. The cobbler decided
to take the risk. But where could he hide the emperor in his
one-room shop? Half the room served as his work area, and
the other half contained a small fire-stove, a table and chair,
and a heap of straw with a sheet on top that served as a bed.

The cobbler rushed forward and removed the sheet. He
parted the straw in the middle, and suggested that the emperor
lie there. He covered the emperor with the straw, flung the
sheet on top, and returned to his work. He was mending
shoes, as if nothing had happened, when the police arrived.

As Frederick expected, the hunt had begun. Policemen and
soldiers were examining each house methodically. They
pushed the cobbler's door open and began searching. "We're
looking for Frederick the Great," they shouted. "He is
dressed in tattered clothes."

The cobbler looked surprised. He gestured toward his room
and said, "No one is here. See for yourself."

The police saw that the cobbler's house was just one room,
that it had no closet or cellar. They felt certain that Frederick
could not hide there. They rushed out and entered the next
house.

The futile hunt lasted two days. Exhausted after searching
everywhere they could think of, the police concluded that
Frederick had escaped. The search ended. Then Frederick
disguised himself differently and left the city.

The cobbler did not wait long before following him. The
very next day, he crept out of the city and was picked up by
Frederick's troops. He asked for an audience with the emperor and was ushered into his presence.

Frederick rushed out to greet him. He embraced the humble cobbler, saying: "You saved my life. Ask me for three things, and, as I promised, they will be granted you."

The cobbler was overwhelmed. He remembered three things that he wanted: a fine house, a large sum of money, and a title. These were given to him.

Then the cobbler thought of a question he had meant to ask the emperor in the beginning. What harm could there be in asking the question now and continuing a friendly chat? He turned to Frederick and said: "Pray, emperor, may I ask you one more thing?"

Frederick was not pleased. He had fulfilled his promise. What else did this Jew want? Remembering, however, the cobbler's risk and that he had saved his life, he replied hesitantly, "What is it?"

"Please tell me," the cobbler asked, "how did you feel when you lay in the straw while the police were looking for you?"

Frederick was white with rage. "You cursed Jew, you dare remind me of this! You will die for your insolence!"

Turning to some soldiers, Frederick ordered them to hang him.

The cobbler was paralyzed with fright. He had had all his heart's desires. Now he was going to die. He felt as if he were falling, as in a dream, falling without an end.

Then, as the soldiers tied the rope about his neck, Frederick approached and stopped the hanging.

The cobbler was led from the gallows. Frederick embraced him. "I could not kill you," he said. "You saved my life."

The cobbler fainted. When he recovered, he cried: "I don't understand. One moment you order my death. The next moment you thank me for saving your life."

"Why don't you understand?" Frederick replied, "I was only answering your question. You wanted to know how I felt when death faced me in your home. Had I tried to tell you, you would not have understood. Here I was Frederick the

Great, emperor of Prussia, and then I was about to die like a
dog. Only when you went through the experience yourself
could you know how I felt. Words cannot substitute for
reality.''

COMMENT

''Before a man eats and drinks, he has two hearts. After he
has partaken of food and drink, he has but one heart,'' states
the Talmud.

The legend about Frederick and the cobbler may provide
the key that will unravel this mysterious talmudic saying.

Before a man eats and drinks, he experiences hunger and
thirst; thus he feels with two hearts: for himself and for others
in distress. He feels the hunger that others suffer. After he
has food and drink, he no longer feels for those in need. He
has only one heart.

Mere words are no substitute for the actual experience of
anguish.

GREED

What a Little Silver Can Do

A Jew named Abraham was famous in Rotterdam for the hospitality he extended to poor wayfarers and itinerant rabbis and preachers. People noted that his name, Abraham, fitted him well, since his practice of hospitality was similar to that of father Abraham (see Genesis 18:2–8).

The Haham of Amsterdam, a noted rabbinic sage, visited Rotterdam one day and stopped at Abraham's home. Abraham was delighted with the distinguished guest and did his utmost to make his visitor comfortable. The Haham noticed that although Abraham was not wealthy, he spared no effort to do all he could for his visitors, often denying necessities to himself and his family. He also observed that even while Abraham was busy with learned guests, he did not overlook the ignorant poor who came begging for alms. He welcomed each with kindness, and all called him brother and friend.

Moved by the dignity of soul he discerned in his host, the Haham put his hands on Abraham's head and blessed him, saying: "May God's blessings be with you in whatever you do."

This prayer, spoken by a grateful, pious man, proved effective. Soon Abraham became one of the wealthiest men in Rotterdam. He was involved in a number of businesses and each was profitable. Although he engaged managers for his many enterprises, he found that his affairs required his personal attention and consumed much of his time. He no longer had opportunities to practice the hospitality for which he was famous. Instead, he designated an executive to care for his charity. This man begrudged the poor their alms and received them roughly. Daily, he decreased their grants until the poor stopped coming altogether.

At that time the Amsterdam Haham needed financial funds for a charitable cause. He sent a special messenger to visit several cities in Holland to collect contributions from co-religionists. When the messenger returned, the Haham inquired how he had been received by Abraham in Rotterdam.

"I was not able to see him," the messenger replied, "People in Rotterdam told me he has changed now that he has come into money. He is no longer hospitable or charitable."

"So my blessing has turned into a curse. I'll have to see what I can do about this," the Haham murmured to himself.

The Haham set out for Rotterdam. Notified of his coming, Abraham met him on his arrival and invited him to his home. He felt instinctively that his wealth was due to the sage's blessing. On entering Abraham's new, well-furnished home the Haham was offered a soft comfortable chair. The Haham was in no rush to be seated. He walked to the window facing the street and looked outside. Abraham joined him.

"Tell me, Abraham, what do you see?" the Haham inquired.

Puzzled at the question, Abraham nevertheless replied, "I see a poor shoemaker."

"And who is that?"

"That is Yentshe, a poor widow who was left with six young children."

Then moving over to a large foyer mirror, the Haham inquired, "Tell me what you see here."

"I see myself," Abraham answered politely but totally perplexed.

"One more question," the Haham persisted; "in what way is this glass different from the glass in your window?"

"The glass is the same," Abraham replied, "except that it has a tint of silver on its back."

"So that's the difference," the Haham sighed. "What a little silver can do!"

Suddenly the meaning dawned upon Abraham. When the glass was without silver, it was transparent. One saw other people through it. But with a tint of silver, one saw only himself in it. And how well this applied to him! When he had little, he loved people, he was very hospitable and charitable. Now that he had come into silver, into wealth, he was absorbed in himself. In the presence of this righteous rabbi, he felt the enormity of his wrongdoing.

"I see that I have done wrong," he burst out sobbing. "I must change my ways! Help me, Haham! Help me go back to my former ways."

"I am glad to hear this," the Haham replied. "Fear not. You will succeed in what you desire. God helps the penitent. I am happy too for another reason. I do not need to revoke my blessing."

The following evening Abraham made a grand feast in honor of his guest. All the townspeople were invited. The poor, especially, were not overlooked. In the midst of the feast Abraham turned to the Haham and said: "I pledge here, before God, that from now on I'll be the same Abraham I formerly was."

COMMENT

King Solomon wisely prayed: "Give me neither poverty nor riches" (Proverbs 30:8). He understood that each can lead man into temptation and sin.

"O cursed lust of gold! When, for thy sake,
The fool throws up his interest in both worlds;
First starved in this, then damned in that to come."
Robert Blair (1699–1746)
The Grave

He Did Not Have to Pay the Doctor

In London a poor Jew found his wife ailing. The family doctor's medicine did not help. Her condition became more serious from day to day. His friends advised him to turn to a prominent specialist as a last resort. He might be able to save her.

Although the specialist was known as one who charged extremely high fees, the Jew felt that he had no alternative but to do all he could to try to save his wife. He visited the doctor, told him about his wife's failing condition, and asked him to treat her.

Looking at the poor man and assuming that he would be unable to pay the usual fee, the doctor was not anxious to accept the new patient.

"This case may involve visits and treatments over a period of weeks," he began to justify his refusal. "I don't believe you can possibly afford to pay for my services."

This reply was not unexpected. The humble Jew was ready to sacrifice all to save his wife.

"If you save my wife, I'll sell my home and pay you every penny of your bill," he said.

"But suppose I cannot save her and she dies, will you still pay me for my services?" asked the avaricious physician.

"I promise you that I will pay you in full whether you cure her or kill her," the agitated husband declared with tears in his eyes.

The doctor accepted the patient and began to visit and treat her. After three weeks, however, the woman passed away.

36

The very next day, the heartless doctor sent her mourning husband a bill for two thousand pounds sterling.

As the Jew was in no hurry to pay the bill, the doctor sued him. The Jew consulted his rabbi. He told the rabbi exactly what had transpired, word for word, when he visited the doctor requesting that he treat his wife. What should he do now? If the doctor won, he would be left penniless.

The rabbi listened sympathetically to the story and gave his advice. The Jew left the rabbi comforted and confident.

When the case was heard in court, the doctor told how he had been engaged by the Jew and how he had been promised to be paid in full no matter what happened, "whether you cure her or kill her." As he concluded his testimony, the judge asked the Jew if he had any questions to ask the plaintiff.

"Yes, your honor," the Jew replied. "I have two questions to ask. The learned doctor told the truth. I did promise him in these words, 'I will pay you in full whether you cure her or kill her.' Question number one: Did you cure my wife? Question number two: Did you kill my wife?"

Laughter broke out in all parts of the courtroom as the Jew completed his argument: "Since he did not cure my wife or kill her, why should I have to pay him?"

The case was dismissed.

COMMENT

The ancient sacred writings of Judaism contain many aphorisms that demonstrate the folly of the greedy man whose desire is insatiable.

For example, "He that hasteneth after riches hath an evil eye and knoweth not that want shall come upon him" (Proverbs 28:22). Also, "He that loveth silver shall not be satisfied with silver; nor he that loveth abundance, with increase" (Ecclesiastes 5:9).

Two Men Who Loved Chicken

There lived a man in Medina with an unusual liking for chicken. His wife satisfied his appetite by preparing a chicken meal for him daily. She would only vary the form of preparation. One day she served boiled chicken, the following day fried, then broiled, afterwards roasted, next baked, and so forth and so on.

This man would leave his home in the morning to attend to his business and return in the afternoon, after a short workday, to find the table set with a delectable chicken dinner displayed appetizingly, waiting for him. He spent the rest of the day in leisure.

One day, as he was enjoying his usual dinner, there was a knock at his front door.

"Who's there?" he called without moving from his seat.

"I am a poor man. I am hungry. Will you please give me some food—even a little—to keep me alive?" the stranger pleaded.

"Go away!" the feasting man growled, angry at being disturbed. "I have nothing to give you. There isn't enough."

"Please, I haven't eaten for three days. Please, give me only a piece of bread or I may die from hunger, please," the beggar pleaded.

The man was disturbed and angry. He rose from his seat, rushed to the door, opened it, and pushed the beggar, to drive him from his house. The push was enough to throw the starving man down to the ground in a faint.

With the words "That was coming to him," the man re-

38

turned to his chicken just as quickly as he had previously risen, but no longer disturbed.

Things changed after that day. The man tried to continue his usual practices. However, instead of gaining money, he would lose it. Soon he lost all he had. He tried to find other employment, but without success. Then he had to sell the furnishings of his home for food, then the home itself. Last to go were the chicken dinners. He had spoken the truth to the beggar: "There isn't enough." In time, as usually happens in these situations, he began to blame his wife for his misery and decided to divorce her.

The wife saw the "hand of God" in what had transpired, accepted her lot, and returned to her parents' home as a divorcee.

Several months passed and she was introduced to a man who was well thought of in her community. They kept company for a short time, found that they had much in common, loved one another, and married.

Now it should come as no surprise that this man's habits were similar to those of her first husband. He also loved chicken. He would also leave in the morning to attend to his business and then, after a short working day, return home in the early afternoon for the rest of the day. His wife found it easy to accommodate him. She had to change very little and they lived happily.

About three months after their marriage, while they were both seated at the dinner table, ready to eat their chicken, there was a knock at the front door.

"Who's there?"

"I am a poor man. I am very hungry. I have not eaten for three days. Please give me some food."

Hearing this the husband rose, took his plate with the hot chicken, heaped several slices of bread on top, and giving it to his wife he asked her to hand it to the hungry stranger. The woman did as she was asked. When she returned, tears were streaming down her face.

"Why are you crying?" the husband asked in astonishment. "Is it because I gave away the chicken you prepared
for me? Don't be foolish. I can eat some herring too for a
change. Why are you crying? Tell me."

The woman did not want to reply. But her husband insisted.
She told him then about her first marriage, what her first
husband had done under similar circumstances, and all that
had happened thereafter. "And now I found *him* to be the
beggar at our door, and when I saw him so humbled, I could
not help but cry."

"Now that you have told me this," the husband said, "I'll
tell you the end of the same story. A part you don't know. I
am the beggar that your first husband refused, knocking me
to the ground. I fell in a faint. When I came to, I murmured a
prayer, 'Almighty God, give me daily bread and spare me the
need for alms. Let me give alms to others.' After uttering this
prayer, I felt new strength coming into my body. Since that
day, fortune has smiled upon me. My prayer was answered.
God turned the tables for your first husband and for me."

COMMENT

"The Lord maketh poor and maketh rich;
He bringeth low, He also lifteth up.
He raiseth up the poor out of the dust,
He lifteth up the needy from the dung-hill,
To make them sit with princes,
And inherit the throne of glory."

—I Samuel 2:7–8

A Just Demand

A wealthy Jew who lived in Sofia was a notorious miser. He never participated in any charitable undertaking of the Jewish community.

His neighbors tried to analyze his stinginess. "This man must think that he will live forever or that he will take his wealth to the grave."

One day the man became very ill. His family spent a small fortune on doctors and specialists trying to get him well, without success. After he died, his family turned to the *Chevrah Kadisha*, the Jewish burial society, and asked them to arrange his burial. It was then that the family was shocked to hear the demand that they must pay the equivalent of ten thousand dollars before the burial would be undertaken.

The family was outraged. This was an unheard-of charge for a grave and burial service in a Jewish cemetery. They went to the city magistrate seeking justice. He, in turn, summoned the *Chevrah Kadisha* to the hearing.

When the society's elders arrived, the magistrate asked: "Why do you demand such a high fee? I know that the deceased was not charitable. Is this an act of vengeance against him?

"No, your honor," an old rabbi in the group replied. "It is not a vengeful demand. It is just a demand."

"What do you mean?"

"You see, your honor, we Jews believe in resurrection, that the dead will come back to life in the future. When we sell a plot of ground in our cemetary, we only rent it until the time of the resurrection. Now this deceased never gave any charity in his lifetime. We do not believe he will be resurrected. Accordingly, we have to sell the grave for all eternity, and that is why we are charging the family such a high fee.''

The magistrate was pleased with the explanation. ''Yours, indeed, is a just demand,'' he decided.

The family had no choice but to pay the full amount that was asked.

COMMENT

Will Durant, in his book *The Age of Faith*, makes this observation: ''No Jew is known to have died of hunger while living in a Jewish community. . . . Christians . . . tried to stir Christians to charity by citing the exemplary generosity of the Jews.''

Only on rare occasions did the Jewish community have to use wise stratagems like the one depicted in this legend to bring a recalcitrant Jew in line.

Beware of Worry

In Salonika a wealthy merchant would regularly pass a poor tailor's shop while going to his business and on returning home. Both were Jews and knew one another. The merchant would see the tailor working and singing at all hours of the day, early in the morning, midday, and at nightfall.

The two were a striking contrast. The poor tailor worked the entire day to earn the barest necessities of life for himself and his family. Yet he was happy, content, singing, and without worry. The well-to-do merchant could easily afford the finest luxuries of life, but he knew no happiness. His appetite was poor and he did not enjoy his food; he did not sleep well at night; he worried constantly and never sang. For he felt he had no reason to sing. Occasionally he would stop and gaze enviously at the tailor, musing, "Here is a man without a single worry! I'd be better off if I could change places with this tailor!"

One day, his mind made up, he decided to try an experiment. He called the tailor to his home.

"I want to ask you a few questions. Maybe I can help you," the merchant began when the tailor was seated at his side, wondering why he had been asked to come. "Tell me, do you really make a living at your work?"

"Thank God, I have no complaints. I have what I need. My work provides me with a living," was the reply of the satisfied man.

"But wouldn't you like to be rich, to have money, to be

43

able to do things that you could never afford to do before?'' the merchant asked.

"I don't know of anyone who would refuse money. If someone wanted to present me with money, I'd be glad to take it. Why not?" the tailor laughed.

At this the merchant took out a wallet stuffed with bills of large denominations and handed it to the tailor. "This is yours to keep and do with as you like. You are an honest man. I like you and I'm glad to give you this gift."

The tailor rushed home to share the unusual news with his wife and children. They counted the money. It was a larger sum than they had ever seen before. What should they do with all this money? Where should they keep it and hide it? There were many things to think about. Surely the tailor did not need to work anymore. But what would he do?

Furthermore, how could he be sure that thieves would not break into his home and rob him of his riches? How could he invest part of the money so that it would double in a short time?

The tailor was filled with worries. He lost his appetite; he did not sleep well anymore; his singing, too, stopped.

After several weeks the tailor lost considerable weight, was restless, nervous, always fidgety. He became a different man.

"What has become of me?" he asked himself in bewilderment one day as he lay shaking in bed. He put his hands on his head and began thinking. "I have lost the joy of living. I'm miserable. I feel like I'm going to die." Then he was able to diagnose his case. "My trouble began when I accepted the money. For me, the money was a curse!" He rose from his bed, snatched the wallet from its hiding place, and brought it back to the merchant.

"Here is your wallet," he said. "It gave me only worry and sickness. Joy and worry, I learned, are incompatible. I'd rather return to my own way of life. I want to be happy and sing again."

COMMENT

This legend demonstrates the truth of such well-known ancient maxims as "Sweet is the sleep of a laboring man, whether he eats little or much; but the satiety of the rich will not let him sleep" (Ecclesiastes 5:11) and "the more property, the more anxiety" (Ethics of the Fathers 2:8).

The ancient rabbis picturesquely described worry as "a yoke of iron upon one's neck" (Jerusalem Talmud, Shabbat 14:3).

Another Tragedy

An elderly gentleman, confined to bed with a grave illness, felt his end approaching. He had his rabbi called to his bedside. He wanted to unburden himself, to make a confession.

When the rabbi arrived, the man revealed his life story and his utter disillusionment with life. Haltingly, in a subdued voice, he outlined the barest facts of his life. He had arrived in Mexico City sixty years before as a child ten years old. His parents had been poor and could not afford to give him a good education. He had spent his entire life in hard work and toil. He had never allowed himself time off from work for any pleasures or vacations.

Somehow, perhaps through his subconsciousness, he had sensed that there were higher ideals in life, more important than money. He had heard that some people derive spiritual strength from attending synagogue; others delight in lending a helping hand to the needy and unfortunate; still others take pleasure in study. But he had postponed these matters.

"When I retire," he had resolved again and again, "when I amass a fortune, then I will devote myself to the synagogue, then I shall lend a helping hand, then I will study. And the tragedy of it all," he continued after a slight pause, "is that just as I was about to retire, finally satisfied with the fortune I have made, just as I was getting ready to carry out these fine projects, I fall ill and I am confined to bed. All my life has been in vain. It's not fair! It's not fair!

These words were his final words. Even before the rabbi

46

had a chance to make a comforting reply, the man's face turned white, his breathing stopped, and he was dead.

COMMENT

This is not an isolated tragedy. It is repeated frequently in modern times. Life's tempo is not conducive to humanitarian and spiritual activities. Many apply the deadly morphine of delay to their live consciences, saying: "Tomorrow, I will get to it. I will do as much as the next fellow and more." But tomorrow never comes.

The Talmud relates that Rabbi Eliezer preached: "Repent one day before your death." His disciples asked: "But does a man know the day he will die?" The sage retorted: "Indeed! Repent today lest you die tomorrow; and all your days should be in penance. King Solomon said, 'Let your garments be white at all times' " (Shabbat 153a).

Brass Buttons

A Chinese prince desired to send a gift of some very costly gems to a neighboring prince.

Whom could he trust with the treasure? After careful consideration, he devised the following strategem. He called his devoted friend and asked him to undertake the mission. The prince was reluctant to reveal the true value of the gift, so he told his friend that he was giving him some brass buttons he had inherited, an heirloom with no value except to his own family. They were a suitable gift for the neighboring prince, who had expressed a desire to have them to remember their friendship.

Saying this, the prince felt sure that his treasure would be safe. There was no temptation to steal them.

However, something unforeseen happened. The friend agreed to fulfill the request. The prince packed the gems in a little box and gave it to him. But no sooner had he left on his journey than he was attacked by a robber who stripped him of all his belongings, including the prince's treasure.

Empty-handed and despondent he returned to his master to report the loss.

"Your Highness," he said on seeing the prince, "I regret to tell you that I was robbed and your brass buttons too were taken from me."

"Fool," the prince cried out on hearing the frightening news, "brass buttons, you say! They were the costliest gems in all China. Why didn't you take along weapons to defend my treasure?"

"Oh, Your Highness," the friend wept, "if you had only told me that in the beginning, I would have taken along weapons to defend your treasure, even with my life. But I thought they were only brass buttons."

COMMENT

A similar situation exists in Jewish life today. Many children receive only a very elementary and fragmentary Jewish education, consisting primarily of reading, writing, and language. They know Judaism only as "brass buttons" and don't understand the precious spiritual treasure that inheres in it. Is it any wonder that some of these youth stray, following the trends of the times, and widen the gap between the generations?

GOD'S WAY

Had Gadya, Had Gadya

In the seventh century, the sultan of Algeria appointed a Jew, Isaac of Algiers, as palace steward.

Reb Isaac, as he was known to his coreligionists, was very charitable. He was fond of inviting the poor to his home for Sabbath and holiday meals, especially the Passover Seder.

One day Reb Isaac was summoned by the sultan, who informed him that his daughter had become engaged to a neighboring prince, with the marriage to take place within six months. Reb Isaac was ordered to obtain the bride's trousseau as well as new garments for the sultan's family. The wedding was to be remembered as the highlight of his reign. Reb Isaac was told that he should spend a specific enormous amount of money for this purpose.

Reb Isaac contacted firms in France and England to order the finest cloths, linens, and silk that were available. He arranged with the best tailors and seamstresses in Algeria to devote their full time to the sultan's needs as soon as the ordered goods arrived. He advanced substantial sums of money in making these orders and arrangements.

When the holiday of Passover approached, Reb Isaac found that he was short of money. Under the circumstances, how would he be able to continue with his yearly custom? Some poor people had already stopped him in the street, intimating that they expected to be his guests for the coming festivities. He did not know what to reply. At night he tossed in his bed and could not sleep. In the morning his mind was made up.

53

He would go to the sultan, tell him of his predicament, and ask to be reimbursed for the advance payments he had made.

Reb Isaac found the sultan in a depressed mood. But he had no choice but to reveal his purpose in coming.

"I also wanted to see you today," the sultan replied. "I have a serious problem. My signet ring is missing. I feel certain it was stolen by someone in my palace. I feel certain, too, that you are the only one who can find it for me. Now, I'll tell you what I'll do. I'll give you the money you requested, and I give you one week to find my ring. If you fail me, you forfeit your life."

Reb Isaac was frightened. He knew that the sultan's words were not an idle threat. He knew the cruelty of this despot. But then another thought entered his mind. The meritorious deed of affording festive Seder meals for so many poor people, this great *mitzvah*, will surely be a protective shield for him.

"I'll do what I can to find your signet ring," he replied.

Over the next three days Reb Isaac was busy preparing for the holidays meals. More than one hundred poor men, women, and children were invited as guests. He arranged for comfortable seating and delicious holiday food and drink. He would think about the sultan's ring after the two Seder meals were past.

Now the sultan had a vizier named Gadya, who was an anti-Semite. He begrudged the honor that the sultan had bestowed upon Reb Isaac. It was he who had devised the devilish threat against Reb Isaac, hoping that it would do away with the Jew for good.

On the night of Passover the vizier, Gadya, was at the sultan's palace slandering the Jews. He said to the sultan: "And how do you think this Jew, Isaac, is celebrating his holiday tonight? He isn't trying to find your signet ring."

"I would like to see what he is doing," the sultan replied.

They disguised themselves, rode to the Jew's house, and peered through his window.

To their surprise they saw Reb Isaac's house well lighted, with a large crowd seated at festive tables ornate with beautiful dishes, cutlery, and flasks filled with sparkling wine. The men were dressed in long white garments with white caps; they were singing happily and appeared to the two spectators as angels. The sultan and his vizier could hardly recognize Reb Isaac, seated at the head of the table in his holiday outfit.

The sultan was favorably impressed by what he saw and heard. He was filled with curiosity and was reluctant to leave. Suddenly they heard Reb Isaac singing, and all the others present joined in the singing again and again, "Had Gadya, Had Gadya." (This is the lullaby poem sung at the close of the Seder.)

The vizier turned white with fright. Isaac of Algiers, he thought, had learned that he had stolen the sultan's ring, and all the "angels" were pointing at him, "That Gadya, that Gadya." He fell to the ground in a faint.

Seeing his vizier in this condition, the sultan realized its meaning. Grabbing the vizier by the neck and slapping him across the face, he revived him and cried, "Tell the truth or you die."

"Yes, I'm guilty. I stole your ring. It is in my house in the closet."

The next day the vizier received the punishment he had intended for the Jew. He was hung in the public marketplace on the outskirts of the city.

COMMENT

That the evil one intends for others may recoil upon oneself is depicted in the story of Haman in the Book of Esther, as well as in a number of biblical maxims, such as the following: "He dug a pit, and hallowed it, and is fallen into the ditch which he made" (Psalms 7:16) and "The righteous is delivered out of trouble, and the wicked cometh in his stead" (Proverbs 11:8).

Man's Limited Mind

The Bible states that the prophet Elijah ascended to heaven while he was still alive (II Kings 2). In Jewish legends, he returns sometimes, as he did in the third century of the common era to Rabbi Joshua ben Levi.

One day Rabbi Joshua urged Elijah to let him accompany him for several days. He wanted to see what Elijah did while he was on earth. Elijah was loath to accede to his request. "You'll ask too many questions, and I cannot be bothered," Elijah insisted. When Rabbi Joshua promised not to ask any questions, Elijah let the rabbi accompany him on his wanderings.

It was not long before Rabbi Joshua regretted his promise. Elijah's deeds were so peculiar: contrary to reason and justice.

On the first night the two wanderers arrived at the hut of a very poor elderly couple whose only worthwhile possession was a cow. The couple received their guests with warm hospitality. They gave them all their food. They offered them their own beds in which to sleep, while they slept on some straw on the floor of their kitchen. In the morning they gave their visitors breakfast with milk they had just drawn from their cow.

When leaving this poor but hospitable couple, Rabbi Joshua overheard Elijah murmur a prayer that the cow would die. The rabbi looked back and saw the cow fall dead. Why should this happen to these charitable people?

The second night, the wanderers came to the mansion of a

wealthy miser. He refused them food and shelter. After they pleaded with him, he allowed them to sleep on the straw in the barn. In the morning, as they were leaving, Rabbi Joshua saw Elijah look back at one mansion wall that seemed curved and about to cave in. He saw him murmur a prayer. He listened intently. To his utter amazement he heard him pray that the wall straighten up, erect and firm. The prayer was answered in a moment. The wall was no longer in danger of falling.

Rabbi Joshua could no longer restrain himself. "I give up," he exclaimed. "You may not take me along any more, but I have to ask you for an explanation. Tell me, why did you kill the poor people's cow and repair the rich miser's wall?"

"The answer is simple," said Elijah. "I saw that the poor woman was destined to die that day. So I prayed that the cow might die in her stead. As for the rich miser, I saw that a great treasure was hidden under the curved wall. Had it fallen, he would have found it. Now that the wall is firm, the treasure will not be disclosed in his lifetime."

COMMENT

Man's limited faculties make him a poor judge of what is a misfortune and what is a blessing.

Solomon decries man's blindness in Proverbs 1:20, 21, 22.

"Wisdom cries aloud in the street,
She raises her voice in the broad places;
She calls at the head of the noisy streets,
At the entrances of the gates,
Uttering her words in the city:
'How long, you thoughtless, will you love thoughtlessness?' "

A Thoughtless Complaint

Persian Jews preserved this simple ancient legend.

In the beginning, when God created the birds, He formed them without wings. They trotted, bounced, and jumped over the surface of the earth as other animals do. They liked being like everyone else, walking and mixing with them.

In time wings began to sprout and grow on their backs. The birds were embarrassed and complained: "Why do we need this appendage? It's a burden to carry!"

One day, when the wings were fully grown, one bird spread them and began to fly. The other birds followed its example. Then, as they floated and soared, the birds realized that the wings were not a burden at all, but a blessing from a kind Providence that gave them buoyance and lift and made it possible for them to soar heavenward, serenely and without care.

COMMENT

People complain about their religion, saying that its laws and precepts are difficult and burdensome. They fail to realize that the observant feel no burden, for religion gives their life meaning and blessing.

The Wall Answered His Prayer

After the Six-Day War, when Israel became larger and Jerusalem, for the first time in nineteen centuries, was a united
city under Jewish control, thousands of tourists flooded Israel
to tour the new territories and especially to visit the Old City
of Jerusalem and the Western Wall (formerly called the Wail-
ing Wall).

Among the tourists who arrived at Lod airport, there was
one who had not come to tour the Holy Land. This Jew from
Switzerland had a different purpose. He came to seek his
eighteen-year-old son.

For the past three or four years the son had expressed an
overwhelming desire to emigrate to Israel. The father, on the
other hand, made light of the matter and endeavored to prove
to the young man, with reason and at times with threats, that
it was better for him to remain in Switzerland. Then one day
the son left home and did not return.

The father futilely hunted everywhere for his son, then
realized that the young man had gone to Israel. After waiting
several weeks for some word from him, that did not come, the
father understood that his son preferred to keep his where-
abouts secret in order to avoid a possible confrontation with
arguments and bitter words.

The father now regretted his stubbornness and longed for
his son. Day and night he thought of his son and wondered
how the youth was managing in Israel. These thoughts gave
him no rest. Finally, one day, he knew he had to go to Israel
to find his son and make peace with him.

59

From Lod airport the father traveled to Tel Aviv, the largest Israeli city. He put advertisements in the newspapers and announcements on the radio. Nothing brought results.

In desperation he went to the Western Wall in Jerusalem. He had heard that many Jews go there to pour out their hearts in prayer, and that some write their prayers on a scrap of folded paper which they put in the cracks between the stones of the Wall. He was prepared to do even this to find his son.

As he first approached the Wall, the last remnant of the Holy Temple structure, he was moved to tears. He recalled the glorious reigns of David and Solomon. He remembered how Jews, including his own parents, had yearned throughout the long years of their exile for the restoration of Zion and the rebuilding of the Holy Temple. He was more fortunate than his parents. He had lived to witness the Proclamation of the State of Israel and now beheld the reunited Holy City of Jerusalem with its ancient sacred sites. He took a prayerbook from his pocket and read some prayers with moist eyes. He thought of his son and tears flowed freely.

Wiping the tears and doing his best to control himself, he took a pen and a piece of paper from his pocket and wrote a few words: "God help me find my son!" After a moment of hesitation and with a heart full of contrition, he added: "I promise not to ask him to leave the Holy Land." He folded the paper and stretched out his hand to place it in a crevice before him.

As he shoved the paper into the crack, another paper was displaced, fell out, and was blown by the wind several feet away. He rushed to get it and put it back in place. As he picked it up, the wind unfolded the paper. He glanced at the writing and recognized it. Trembling he read the words: "Forgive me, God, that in my love of this land I caused my father pain." The signature and address that followed were those of his son!

That same day father and son were happily reunited.

COMMENT

This story was reported in an Israeli newspaper on November 11, 1969. Regrettably, it was not given the conspicuous place and full treatment that it deserved.

Parents may wisely learn from this almost legendary story to give due consideration to the requests of their children, and not think only of their own convenience. The desires of children are not always childish.

There is a still greater moral inherent in this extraordinary event. It bids man never to give up hope.

As the Talmud expressed it: "Even if a sharp sword rests upon a man's neck, he should not desist from prayer."

A Dead Monkey Brought Him Gold

A pious but poor tailor called Reb Moshe lived in Afghanistan. He worked half a day. The remaining part of the day and much of the night he studied Talmud and other holy books. Because he was a skilled worker, the prince of Afghanistan hired him, with the understanding that he would devote his working hours to the needs of the prince and his family.

The arrangement continued satisfactorily for several years.

One year, about ten days before the Passover holiday, the prince's wife suggested that he reward the tailor. "Since the Jewish holiday is approaching, it would be nice if you would give him some extra money. Let him celebrate his holiday more joyfully and know that we appreciate his fine workmanship."

The prince liked the suggestion and summoned the tailor to the palace.

"Listen," the prince addressed Reb Moshe on his arrival. "Your holiday is coming and you will need money to celebrate it." The prince held up a bill of a large denomination and continued: "I'm giving this to you. I want you to know that if not for me, you and your family would have starved to death long ago."

At first Reb Moshe was pleased to see the gift. But he felt that the last words were blasphemy, and he could not keep silent.

"Your honor," he replied respectfully, "what you say is not entirely correct. It is true that I have earned my livelihood from you for the last several years. However, this does not mean that you kept us from hunger. Our Father in heaven takes care of those who trust in Him.''

The prince was angered: ''You ungrateful Jew,'' he hollered, ''I should fire you and see if your Father in heaven will take care of you.''

The prince's wife was surprised by the sudden outburst. She did not want to lose the tailor who performed such fine handiwork for her.

''Reb Moshe,'' she said, ''apologize to the prince and all will be forgotten.''

''I have no reason to apologize. I stated my firm belief. God in His mercy provides for those who put their trust in Him,'' Reb Moshe replied.

''You are fired!'' the prince thundered in wrath. ''You are no longer our tailor. Let us see how long your God will keep you alive.''

When Reb Moshe returned home, his wife and children bewailed the news. ''How will we provide for the Passover holiday?'' his wife lamented.

Reb Moshe comforted her. ''Don't worry,'' he said, ''God will not forsake us.'' He now applied more time to his sacred books.

With each passing day, food became more scarce. The woman was at her wit's end, not knowing where the food for the next day would come, leave alone the special items needed for the Passover holiday. Reb Moshe, however, was totally absorbed in his studies. Not a shadow of worry crossed his countenance.

The food was gone two days before the holiday. The wife put her children to bed hungry and crying. She too wept silently. Reb Moshe, however, was unmoved. ''God will help,'' he said with assurance.

That night the window pane in their front room was violently shattered by a loud thud that awakened the poor woman with fright. Even her husband, who was absorbed in his studies, was shaken.

"What happened!" each shrieked in terror.

Taking a candle, Reb Moshe crept cautiously into the front room. Bits of glass were scattered over the floor. Then, in the frightening shadow of the candlelight, in the middle of the room he saw a carcass stretched across the floor.

"O God!," he trembled, "is this another of those blood accusations before the Passover holiday?"

He approached the body and was relieved to find that it was not a human being. It was a dead monkey.

"Some vicious person was trying to frighten us," he told his wife.

Reb Moshe took the carcass by its tail to toss it outside into the garbage pail. He heard a coin drop. He lowered the monkey to the floor, picked up the coin, and examined it by the candlelight. It was gold. "It fell from the monkey's mouth," he told his wife. "This monkey may have more coins in its stomach."

His wife agreed that this was likely. She brought a knife from the kitchen, and Reb Moshe split the monkey's stomach. They were right. The stomach was filled with gold coins. They were rich. They prepared a festive Passover the next day.

That night the family celebrated the Seder at a table adorned with expensive embellishments they had never enjoyed before. Suddenly there was a knock at the door. When one of the children opened the door, the family was surprised to see the prince and his wife.

"We came to see how your God provided for you," explained the prince.

Reb Moshe invited his guests to the table. The prince was amazed at what he saw: the decorations, the table setting, the embroidered tablecloth, the candles in a silver candelabra, the gold goblets filled with sparkling wine, the matzos and fine dishes.

"Tell me the truth. Where did you get all this? We did not expect to find all of this," the prince inquired in a subdued tone.

"I'll tell you the truth, honored guests," Reb Moshe replied. "I'll hide nothing from you. It is a very strange story." And he told them what had happened and how he got the gold coins. "This is how God provided us with all our needs," he ended the tale.

The prince listened in amazement. Then, rousing himself, he gave his coachman the names of two palace servants and ordered him to bring them at once. When the two servants arrived, shaking in fright, the prince asked them, "Tell me, what did you do with the dead monkey I told you to dispose of?"

"Your honor, forgive us," they humbly replied. "We thought we would play a prank on this Jew whom you fired. We threw the monkey through his window."

"I understand now what happened," explained the prince. "I had wondered about my monkey. It was suddenly seized with convulsions and died before we could call a veterinarian. Later I saw that many of my gold coins had disappeared and wondered who could have stolen them. I understand now.

"The monkey saw me putting gold coins between my teeth to test them, to determine if they were genuine. He must have thought that they were good to eat. Two days ago, I left the monkey alone in my office for about ten minutes. I had to step out to attend to some business. The monkey must have taken some gold coins and swallowed them. Yes, Reb Moshe, I see now that you're right. God did provide you with all your needs for your holiday. I'm not going to take back what God gave you! You keep the coins that you found in the monkey. After the holiday, Reb Moshe, come back to my palace. Please. I'd like you to be our tailor."

COMMENT

Reb Moshe's faith is portrayed in the Book of Psalms: "But as for me, in Thy mercy do I trust; my heart shall rejoice in Thy salvation" (13:6).

Similarly, "In Thee did your fathers trust; they trusted, and Thou didst deliver them" (22:5); "The Lord is my strength and my shield, my heart trusted in Him and I was helped" (28:7); and "Commit yourself to the Lord; trust in Him, and He will bring it to pass" (37:5).

The Cure for Insomnia

(The author heard this story several years ago in Israel from the Costa Rican Jew who underwent this experience. He attempts to retell it here as he heard it.)

Two years ago, on my seventieth birthday, I had to undergo a serious operation. Fortunately the operation was successful and I made a rapid recovery. However, during the convalescence, I noticed that I did not sleep well. The doctor gave me different kinds of sleeping pills, but they did not help. In fact, the situation worsened. It seemed as if I did not sleep at all.

During the sleepless nights when I tossed in bed, I tried to figure out why I could not sleep. Gradually I began to understand. I said to myself, if a man has to take a sea voyage for the first time, he probably will be unable to sleep a night or two before the trip. Similarly, the same phenomenon would occur to one taking an airplane trip for the first time. Now, since I am seventy years old and have reached the biblical span of three-score years and ten, and since I'll soon have to undertake a trip into the great beyond, is it any wonder that I cannot sleep?

My diagnosis seemed to make sense. Yet, while the analysis gave me a certain amount of intellectual satisfaction, I still could not sleep.

It occurred to me then that it might help if I would write to my son who was taking a postgraduate course in a New York City rabbinical school. I would tell him about my problem and ask him to discuss the matter with some of his teachers.

Hopefully they would have a remedy. My son, eager to fulfill the Fifth Commandment, "Honor thy father and thy mother," was quick in complying with my request. He sent me his teacher's reply. The advice was to read a religious book until I become drowsy. This teacher was a *Hasid*, a follower of the teachings of Rabbi Nahman of Bratzlav. My son purchased a copy of Rabbi Nahman's *Sefer Hamidot*, a book of ethical meditations, and enclosed it with his reply.

I began reading it that same evening. I noticed that the topics were arranged alphabetically. I wondered whether the topic "sleep" was included in the book. I turned to that letter and found that one page was devoted to the subject. The first paragraph stated that most people could sleep less without harm to their health. That did not apply to me. I could barely sleep at all. I read on. And here it was: "If a man finds that it is difficult to sleep, let him think of the resurrection."

As I read those words, I was overwhelmed. I shook from head to foot. I thought: This saint diagnoses my problem just as I did. There is only one difference. I was thinking of death as a one-way trip, but he advises us to think of it as a two-way trip, with the resurrection as the return trip. This advice had a good effect on me. I have never suffered from sleeplessness again.

COMMENT

Jews believe in two kinds of resurrection: individual and national. Jews have been mocked because of their faith in both. How can an individual long dead, whose body is decayed and decomposed, come to life again? And similarly, how can a people driven from its homeland for almost two thousand years, and scattered throughout the world, revive on its ancestral soil? Such a thing had never happened, yet Jews throughout history clung steadfastly to their belief in the two resurrections divinely promised through the prophets.

In 1948, with the Proclamation of the State of Israel, one of these beliefs was vindicated. The national resurrection of the Jewish people began. What was it that assured the survival of the people? Perhaps here, too, Rabbi Nahman's remedy proved effective. The faith of the Jews in the divine promise of return saved them from despair, death, and oblivion.

UNDERSTANDING LIFE

"I'll Never Forgive That Doctor!"

In a small Austrian town a man was seized with hiccups. The doctors advised his family that the hiccups might stop if he was frightened suddenly. The family tried and failed. The patient continued hiccupping, lost weight, and was confined to bed.

One day, his family heard that the Emperor Franz Joseph, who was touring the country, was scheduled to visit the town. They pleaded with the town officials to petition the emperor to permit the royal physician to examine the patient. The request was granted and the family was overjoyed.

When the doctor arrived, he stood in the open door of the bedroom to catch a glimpse of the patient. There, in the hearing of everybody, including the invalid, he shouted: "How dare you waste my time! Can't you see that he is dying!"

The patient was so shocked that he paled, stopped hiccupping, and was cured.

Thereafter, he would always say: "I'll never forgive that doctor! He almost frightened me to death!"

COMMENT

This legend illustrates the wisdom of Ecclesiastes: "Be not hasty in thy spirit to be angry, for anger resteth in the bosom of fools" (7:9).

Anger is a grave sin. The Talmud reports that Elijah taught one scholar this advice: "Fall not into anger, and thou wilt not sin" (Berakoth 29b).

King for a Year

A man was on a sea voyage when a terrible storm broke with fierce fury. The ship rose and fell with the waves, and within minutes it was wrecked and splintered. It sunk quickly. He survived, holding on to a board, tossing with the surging waves. For a day and a night the man endured the fury of the sea until he felt his strength ebbing away. He was about to accept his fate and sink into the black oblivion when the waves rose and tossed him tumbling upon the shore of an uncharted island.

He lay on the sand exhausted, almost dead, for a long time. Later, he rose and began to explore the island. He walked for several hours, saw buildings, and realized that the island was large and well populated. He was sighted by some of the natives, who surrounded him and exclaimed: "You are our new king!"

The man was carried into the city on the natives' shoulders, taken to the royal palace, and dressed in gold. Trumpets were sounded and people gathered in the palace courtyard to witness the coronation. With lavish ceremony the man was seated on a lush, golden throne and crowned with a crown of gold and jewels. The people shouted: "Long live our king! Long live our king!"

Hardly able to believe what was happening, the man thought he was dreaming and would soon awake. Yet when he awoke the next morning, he was still lying on silken sheets, and servants were there to help him bathe and dress. A royal breakfast of the finest fruits and other foods was served, and shortly thereafter, splendidly attired government officials visited him and congratulated him and pledged him homage. He was handed the silver palace keys on a golden tray and shown sparkling jewels from the royal treasury. He was assured that he would be consulted regularly for his advice on government affairs.

From all appearances he was king. Yet he was uneasy. He could not understand it. Why would these people take a complete stranger, whose ability they had never tested, and make him their king? He put this question one day secretly to a servant.

"Your Majesty," the servant replied, "this is a secret that our law forbids us to divulge."

The servant's reply alarmed the king. He insisted upon a reply. He pleaded and threatened. He refused to eat or drink. He promised that the servant would not be harmed if he revealed the secret, and offered him a reward. The servant relented. He said: "We crown strangers as king for a year. During that year the king rules the country and can do what he wants. At the end of the year, we take everything from him and dress him in the clothes he wore when he appeared on our island. We take him by ship to a distant desolated island and leave him there to starve."

"Have any of my predecessors taken any precaution to avert this calamity?" the king inquired.

"To tell you the truth," the servant replied, "they were so anxious to enjoy each day's delights that they never asked what might happen tomorrow."

This king acted differently. He gathered a large crew of workers and shipped them to the far-off island to till the soil, to plant trees and gardens. They built a comfortable home there with barns for domestic animals. He transported animals and food, and enough books to last a lifetime.

When the year ended, the king was prepared. He left content with his past and assured about his future. He knew he was not going to a desolate island to starve alone, but to a garden island where he could enjoy life's comforts as long as he lived.

COMMENT

This legend was first quoted in the name of Rabbi Nahman of Horodenka, the devoted disciple and friend of Rabbi Israel Baal Shem Tov, in Miedzyboz, Podolia. It illustrates the possibilities that inhere in life. While many waste their days without thinking of the morrow, the wise person accumulates good deeds every day. These will support him in the hereafter. When his life ends, he can go to his maker unafraid.

"This world is like a vestibule before the world-to-come; prepare yourself in the vestibule, so that you enter the banqueting hall" (Ethics of the Fathers 4:21).

Where Is Happiness?

Isaac Yeklis of Cracow had a dream. He was informed that if he traveled to the courtyard of the king's palace in Prague and dug under the bridge, he would find a great treasure. Isaac Yeklis paid no attention to his dream. A trip to Prague was out of the question. Instead of gaining money, he would lose it. There was a considerable expense involved, as well as time and effort. When his dream kept reappearing night after night, however, he realized that it was not an ordinary dream. It was a prophetic vision.

Isaac Yeklis undertood the trip. After many days and many hardships, he reached the capital and rented a cheap room at an inn close to the king's palace. He rose early the next morning and rushed optimistically to the palace courtyard. But he found no way to dig under the bridge without being seen. The palace was guarded by the finest soldiers in the royal army. Isaac visited the area on different days and at different hours, night and day, and found no change. The guards were there constantly. It seemed futile to attempt any digging. He was disappointed and felt foolish for having undertaken the trip.

But one morning, as he stood by the bridge, deeply depressed, one of the officers, who had watched him many times, walked over to him and asked what he wanted. Isaac Yeklis realized that he had nothing to lose. He confessed that he had traveled very far because of a prophetic dream's promise that he would find a treasure if he would dig under the bridge near the king's courtyard.

The army officer burst out laughing. "You fool! You wasted time and money because of a dream. I had a similar dream but I wasn't as stupid as you. I didn't leave my job. I didn't waste money. I dreamed that I should travel to Cracow, look for the house of Isaac Yeklis, sneak into the house, dig under the kitchen stove, and there I would find treasure. Do you think I am so stupid as to go hunting phantom treasures in Cracow!"

The officer continued to laugh. He mocked and insulted him.

Isaac Yeklis was startled. He heard his name and city. He realized that his dream had led him to get this message from the officer. He turned, rushed back to Cracow, dug under his stove, and sure enough he found a treasure. He became rich and built a synagogue in Cracow that is still called the Synagogue of Isaac Yeklis.

COMMENT

Isaac Yeklis is the personification of every man and woman. Don't people always dream that their happiness is over there, just beyond their reach, in the king's courtyard? Money-hungry people dream of a million dollars. Others dream of happiness, valuable possessions, a Cadillac each year, a mink coat, diamonds. Some think of a pleasure trip around the world that they cannot afford. Happiness is always over there, beyond reach.

When Isaac Yeklis gave up his dreams, he found happiness at his own hearth. He was able to apply himself to work for an ideal, for a goal. By hard work he was able to make a contribution in building a synagogue.

When the ancient Jewish sage inquired, "Who is rich?" he did not answer, "He who possesses a million dollars." The sage knew that one who possesses a million dollars may be poorer than the poor. He may not have peace of mind or contentment. His appetite has been sharpened and his desires lie still further beyond his grasp. He now craves a hundred million dollars.

The Mistake of a Lifetime

A New York septuagenarian couple visited their rabbi and requested a *get* (the religious divorce required by Jewish law in addition to the civil divorce that may be obtained in the state court).

The rabbi was surprised. "I don't understand why you have come to me. You've always seemed compatible. You've raised a fine family, sons and daughters. We're proud of each of them. Three weeks ago you married off your last child, your daughter, to a fine, respectable young man. What a festive celebration it was! I enjoyed being there. We're still talking about it. All your children, grandchildren, relatives, and friends were there—several hundred people—congratulating you both. It seemed to me that they all echoed the sentiment that I expressed in my sermon that day: 'What a fine, blessed couple you are!' Now you ask for a *get*. I don't understand it! What happened?"

"I'll try to explain," the old man replied. "When we married forty-one years ago, I realized after the first few days that we were not suited to each other. However, we were on our honeymoon, and it seemed the wrong time to talk of divorce. So I waited. Coming home, I learned that my wife was pregnant. Again the time was wrong. How could I divorce her then when my child was growing in her womb? When our son was born she was a nursing mother. I couldn't divorce her in that condition! So I waited. Before I realized it, she was pregnant again. We were blessed in this fashion ten times. So, how could I act. Then there were new things. We had to

80

arrange for Bar Mitzvah and Bas Mitzvah celebrations. Then, as God would have it, some of our children reached marriageable age. A divorce at that time might have had disastrous results on both the older and younger children. How could I hurt them? So I waited. Now, thank God, our children are all married. So we are here to ask you for a *get* to make good the mistake of a lifetime.''

COMMENT

''Any man may make a mistake; none but a fool will persist in it'' Cicero (106–143 B.C.E.) *Phillippicae*. ''Error, wounded, withes in pain'' William Cullen Bryant (1794–1878) *The Battle-Field*. ''A man protesting against error is on the way toward uniting himself with all that believe in truth'' Thomas Carlyle (1795–1881) *Heroes and Hero-Worship*.

Distribute Not Thy Wealth
in Thy Lifetime

An elderly Johannesburg man, well-to-do and highly respected in the community for his goodness and wisdom, discovered to his sorrow that he had done one foolish thing in the declining years of his life.

When his wife, his companion for more than half a century, passed away, his children persuaded him to give up his lavish home and live with one of them. "It isn't good for a man to live alone, especially an elderly man," they argued. They assured him that each had an extra room for him and that it would give them pleasure to make him comfortable and to care for his needs. Persuaded by the apparent reasonableness of the proposal, the old man accepted the offer of his married daughter who had no children. "I think I'll be a smaller burden at your house."

For several months he had no reason to regret his decision. He was treated with love.

One day, however, his children called a meeting. It seemed reasonable to them to alter their proposal. Why should their father keep his wealth in his own name? His needs were taken care of. Why shouldn't he distribute his estate now in his lifetime? He would avoid lawyers' fees and court expenses. He would have the satisfaction of hearing the grateful thanks of his children.

The old father was persuaded again. But this time it did not take long before he realized the folly of his action.

Within weeks, he began to notice a changed atmosphere in

the home. The love and honor that he had enjoyed from his daughter and son-in-law began to defuse and evaporate. His other children forgot him completely. It was only now that his daughter noticed that his hand was shaking and ordered him to eat in the kitchen at the plastic table with the servant girl in order not to mess up her fine tablecloths, really her mother's tablecloths that she had received earlier as an inheritance from her father.

The old man was miserable. He could not eat or sleep. He could not forgive himself for his foolish decision. He had it coming to him! But could anything be done?

One day, as he was strolling in the park disconsolately, an old friend stopped him. "What's happened to you? You've lost so much weight! You look so downcast!"

The old man unburdened himself to his friend.

His friend was touched, and after some moments of reflection said, "I believe I can help you." He devised a plan that entailed his lending the old man a precious stone for a day or two.

That evening, while sitting in the kitchen for supper, the old man playfully fondled a large diamond. His daughter passed by and stopped suddenly! "What is this, father? It looks like an expensive diamond of twelve karats or more!"

"That's true," the old man said. "It's the gift I bought your mother on our fiftieth wedding anniversay. I hoped she would make a ring or a pin of it. She preferred to keep the stone as it is, to look at it from time to time, to admire it and cherish it as a token of our love."

"But father, this stone must have cost you fifty thousand dollars. It's too expensive to carry around. Come into the dining room and let's discuss the matter."

The old may could not be persuaded to part with the stone. All the arguments and flattery tried by his daughter and son-in-law were of no avail. After the lengthy session a compromise was accepted by the father. He would open a safety-deposit box in the neighborhood bank in his own name. He would deposit the diamond for safekeeping there with the proviso that upon his death the contents of the box would be bequeathed to his daughter.

The arrangement worked a miracle. The father was treated thereafter with what seemed like love and respect. His daughter and her husband were careful not to antagonize the old man in any way.

He lived his last years in peace and calm. When he passed away and his daughter obtained the right to open the box and claim its contents, she found no precious stone, but a leather strap with a note in her father's now steady hand: "He who distributes his wealth in his lifetime should be thrashed with this strap!"

COMMENT

These children felt "that the principle duty which a parent owed to a child was to make him happy" Anthony Trollope (1815–1882) *Doctor Thorne*. They forgot to: "Conduct thyself towards thy parents as thou wouldst wish thy children to conduct themselves toward thee" Isocrates (436–338 B.V.E.) *Ad Demonicum*. They sank to the lowest of the three degress of filial piety. "The highest is being a credit to our parents, the second is not disgracing them; the lowest is being able simply to support them" Confucius (c. 551–478 B.C.E.) The Book of Rites.

Woe to parents who must teach their children to obey the Fifth Commandment, "Honor thy father and mother," (Exodus 20:12 and Deuteronomy 5:16) in their old age.

EXPLAINING
SCRIPTURES

The Truly Great Are Immortal

Many years back a small Jewish Romanian community was looking for a rabbi. They heard about a young rabbi who had recently been ordained with honors at a prominent Lithuanian yeshiva. They sent a delegation of three prominent citizens to visit and impress the young scholar and to invite him to become their rabbi.

As with most synagogues, they were unable to offer much financial inducement. The rabbi was not inclined to accept. When the delegation sensed failure, one of the men, more daring than the others, offered another inducement: "Do you know, Rabbi, that some of the most prominent sages and rabbis of the world are buried in our community?"

The rabbi understood the implication. If he accepted the position he would be successor to many distinguished rabbis. Furthermore, after he had completed his life, his earthly remains would repose in the community cemetery alongside his distinguished predecessors.

The rabbi was won over. He accepted the position. Shortly after coming to the community, however, he realized his mistake. His salary was small and he was lonely, not having any learned friends in the community with whom he could speak. One day, when he was especially lonesome, he decided to visit the cemetery and see the names of his predecessors. He walked through the cemetery, examining the monument inscriptions, but found no names that he recognized. He returned home and sent for the officials who had visited him at his school. When the men arrived he said: "Gentlemen, you remember that you assured me that you have some of the most prominent and distinguished rabbis interred in your city. Tell me who are these rabbis, these prominent scholars.''

"Rabbi, in our community the Rambam is buried, also Rashi and the Rema.''

The rabbi was furious: "How dare you say this! Do you think I'm stupid! Everyone knows that the great philosopher Rambam (1135–1204) is interred in Tiberias; Rashi, the most popular expounder of the Holy Bible and the Talmud (1040–1105), is buried in France, and the sepulchre of the Rema, the saintly Rabbi Moses Isserles (1510–1572), is in the city of Cracow.''

The dauntless spokesman answered again: "Rabbi, don't be angry with us. We spoke the truth. You can go to Tiberias and visit their schoolhouses and synagogues and you will see that the Rambam still lives there. He is discussed. His words are studied with great respect. You can go through the Jewish academies of France and you will see that Rashi lives there. Young and old, even those who do not know very much, study his words. He shares the life of everyone who learns the Bible and the Talmud. You can go to Cracow and you will see the Rema alive there. The people live by his rulings, set forth in his Code of Laws. But in our community all three scholars are dead and buried. You will find no one here, neither young nor old, wise nor unlearned, repeating the words of the Rambam, Rashi, or Rema. It is true, rabbi, that in our town each of these Jewish masters is buried!''

COMMENT

The author recalls that as a child he heard a Romanian rabbi preach a sermon in which he used this legend to explain a biblical passage that appeared self-contradictory.

The Bible relates that when Moses died, "he was buried in the valley in the land of Moab over against Bethpeor; and no man knows his sepulchre unto this day'' (Deuteronomy 34:6).

The Bible gives us three specific signs to locate Moses' burial place. He was buried in the valley, in the land of Moab, over against Bethpeor. And yet it concludes that "no man knows his sepulchre unto this day." Doesn't the second half of the verse contradict the first half?

After telling the legend, the rabbi explained the biblical verse: "Where is Moses buried? The Bible tells us. He is buried 'in the valley,' in a place where light does not penetrate, where enlightenment is absent. He is buried 'in the land of Moab,' among primitive, uncivilized people. He is buried 'over against Bethpeor,' idol worshippers who have not studied his teachings. But 'no man knows his sepulchre unto this day.' For anyone worthy of the title 'man,' Moses is not dead. Moses still lives!"

The King Loved Music

An ancient Tunisian despot had a court musician who was unusually adept at playing the violin. As the music filled the palace, the monarch would forget his responsibilities and listen in ecstatic raptures.

The musician, however, was degenerate. Knowing how his talent captivated the ruler, he did not fear to commit all kinds of crimes without hesitation.

When complaints came to the monarch, he dismissed them, giving the criminal only a slight reproof. "I need this man. I love his music," the king would murmur apologetically.

The monarch's condoning attitude emboldened the culprit. He robbed and killed. He forcibly violated married women, even the wives of Tunisia's notables. Loud complaints about his heinous crimes were heard throughout the country, including the palace, but the king was helpless.

One day the husband of one of the raped women decided to administer his own justice. He waited for the violinist near the palace entrance with an ax hidden under his tunic. When the musician appeared, he lifted the ax and brought it down firmly against the violinist's right arm, severing it above the elbow.

The musician crawled back to the throne room bleeding profusely, crying to the monarch, "Look what that man did to me!"

As soon as the monarch understood what had happened, he ordered two guards to drag the bleeding musician to the gallows and hang him publicly for his past crimes.

"Why, your honor?" the condemned man wailed. "When

I committed the acts, you forgave me. Now, when that man cut off my hand, instead of punishing him, you hang me.''

"I never punished you before," the king replied, "because I needed you. I loved your music. It was a great delight. Actually you should have been hanged a dozen times before. However, I could not get myself to forgo the pleasure of your music. But now that your right hand is cut off and you will never play again, you will get the long-due punishment you deserve.''

COMMENT

Some medieval preachers used this legend to explain a seeming contradiction in ancient Jewish sources.

The talmud states that the Holy Temple was destroyed and the people exiled from Israel because of their grave sins (Yoma 9b and Shabbat 33a). In contrast, the prophet Jeremiah attributes these calamities to the people's forsaking the study of Torah (Jeremiah 9:11–12). How are we to reconcile these conflicting statements?

The preachers say there is no contradiction. Both statements are true. Torah study is heavenly music in which God takes great delight. So long as the people continued to study Torah, God was patient with them, hoping, as it were, that the Torah itself would prove an effective antidote for their sins. As the people forsook the study of Torah, however, the heavenly music ceased, and with it the hope for a change in their behavior. The people then received the punishment due for their grave sins.

He Slumbers Not, Nor Sleepeth

During the Middle Ages, and until quite recently, false blood accusations were frequently raised against Jews. The ancient Jewish chronicles report many such incidents during which Jewish communities were savagely plundered and brutally massacred. Sometimes, however, a miracle would occur, the real culprit was found and the Jews were saved. Such a case occurred in Spain during the thirteenth century, in the reign of a just and honorable king.

A few days before Passover, two non-Jews came to complain one morning at the king's palace. They had already spread the word among the masses, and this was only their formal announcement. A large crowd had gathered to make certain that justice was done. The pair claimed that they had found the body of a non-Jew in a Jew's yard. They intimated that the Jews had slain the person to use his blood for the baking of their matzos.

When the king heard the excitement, he appeared on the balcony over the courtyard and ordered silence. He assured the crowd that he himself would render judgment in this case.

The king ordered the witnesses to step forward and had them put under guard. He then sent messengers to summon the Jewish leaders in order that they might see him decide the case fairly and honestly. The defendant, too, was ordered to be brought to the court, and the king gave special orders that no harm was to befall him until the evidence had been heard.

When all arrived, the king asked if there were other witnesses who wished to testify. To the crowd's astonishment, four of the king's guards stepped forward as witnesses. The king requested the two men who had registered the complaint to testify. They said that during the night they had seen the Jew and the non-Jew from a distance walking together and entering the Jew's yard. They waited but did not see the non-Jew leave. That night they could not sleep. They feared that the Jew might try some foul play. In the morning they called some friends, went and opened the Jew's yard, and found the non-Jew lying dead. Surely the Jew must have slain him for some religious purpose.

The king then called upon his four guards to testify.

"Your honor," they said, "last night, just past one o'clock in the morning, you called us and rushed us out into the street. You told us to follow, in hiding, two men who were running and carrying a human body. You asked us to find out, if possible, whether the body they were carrying was alive. You ordered us to see what they would do with the body.

"We followed your instructions. To the best of our knowledge, the body was a corpse. We followed the two men quietly. We saw them approach the Jew's house, the defendant here, open the gate of his yard, drop the dead man there, and dash off. Those two were the two who have just testified before you."

A hush fell in the courtyard as the king began his comments.

Turning to the Jewish elders, who were delighted with the turn of events, he said, "I'd like to ask you something. In the Bible it is written that 'the keeper of Israel slumbers not, nor sleepeth' (Psalms 121:4). To slumber means to sleep lightly, to doze, to drowse. Now, if God slumbers not, surely He does not sleep. Why does the Bible add 'nor sleepeth'? Isn't it superfluous?"

As the elders hesitated, the king proceeded with a smile, "I'll tell you the answer. I learned it last night. I could not fall asleep. I tossed in my bed for hours. I got up and looked through the window, and lo and behold, I saw those two

running with a dead body. You know the rest of the story.
The answer to my question is simple. The keeper of Israel
slumbers not, *nor does He allow others to sleep.*''

COMMENT

New situations in life frequently reveal new meaning in Scriptures that were hidden and unknown.

Jews have never hesitated to accept a new interpretation of
a biblical passage, even from a non-Jew, if it conforms with
their sacred tradition. Such interpretations are reported even
in the Talmud and in the other ancient sacred books of the
Jews, giving their non-Jewish source.

Baruch Ha-Levi Epstein (1860–1942) explains in *Baruch
Sheamar,* p. 5, that Jewish morning prayer begins with the
words of the non-Jewish Jew-hater Balaam from Num 24:5 to
teach, at the onset of the day, that truth is truth no matter
what its source.

MARRIAGE

Three Kinds of Wives

A wealthy man died leaving five sons and a testament that was unclear to them. They decided to seek advice from one of three famous brothers who lived in a far-off Ethiopian town. The three were known for their wisdom. The sons hoped that one of them would be able to explain their father's will and make it possible for them to fulfill his last wishes.

After a long trip, they arrived in the Ethiopian town. On inquiry, they were shown the home of one of the three brothers. When they were admitted, they were surprised to see an extremely old man. His face was wrinkled. His hair was white. His head was bent. His entire body trembled. Could he be of help to them, they wondered. Nevertheless, they told him their problem. After some reflection, he replied haltingly: "I regret, I do not know the answer. You will have to see my older brother."

The five sons were shocked by his reply. This man, they estimated, must be a hundred years old. How could they expect any help from an older man!

Nevertheless, since they had already made the long trip to this town, they figured that it would be foolish to leave without seeing the older brother as the old man suggested.

Later, when they entered the home of the older brother, they were surprised to see that he looked younger then the first. He was grey, with several wrinkles cutting across his face, but otherwise quite erect and vigorous. "This brother looks eighty years old," the five sons thought. They explained the purpose of their visit, but after hearing their request he

97

also replied: "I am sorry, but I do not know the solution to your problem. You will have to visit our oldest brother."

The five sons were more confused. They were certain that their trip was in vain. But they decided to visit the oldest brother before they returned home, if for no other reason, at least to satisfy their curiosity.

They approached this house and knocked on a finely polished door. An elderly woman, neatly dressed, welcomed them. They told her that they wanted to speak to her husband. She explained that he had been taking his afternoon nap, but she would go and see if he was awake. She ascended the stairs softly toward the bedroom. After a while she returned and informed the visitors that her husband would be down momentarily.

As he walked into the room, the visitors were astonished. He was a man who appeared no older then sixty. His hair was only slightly grey. His face was without wrinkles. His body was fully erect. He greeted them warmly and asked if he could help. They informed him of their problem, which he resolved for them. "Wait," he added, as they were about to leave, "I can see on your faces that something else is troubling you. Tell me what it is. Perhaps I can solve this problem for you as well."

The brothers were delighted with this opportunity. They said: "It is true that we are troubled. We visited your two brothers. Both told us that you are the oldest. We can hardly believe it. We would have sworn that the youngest brother is a hundred years old, the middle one eighty, and that you look the youngest, about sixty. Is someone playing a joke on us?"

The wise man told them that they had heard the truth.

"I presume you know," he proceeded, "that there are three kinds of bees in this country. There is the bee that gives honey and bites. There is also the bee that bites and gives no honey. And then there is the bee that gives honey and does not bite. Similarly, there are three kinds of wives. My youngest brother has a wife that is like the bee that bites and gives no honey. That is why he has aged before his time. Our middle brother has a wife that is like the bee that bites but also gives honey. He does not look as old as our youngest brother. I am blessed with a wife that is like the bee that gives honey but does not bite.''

Then, with a sparkle in his eyes, he faced his wife, who was watching him attentively, and added, ''My wife is the secret of my youthfulness!''

COMMENT

What has been said here about wives may also be said of husbands. There are as many different kinds of husbands as there are different kinds of wives. This legend dramatizes the truth that spousal relations can affect physical well-being and longevity. This fact, regrettably, is known and appreciated by too few people.

The wise author of Eccesiasticus knew the truth. He said: ''Blessed is the man that hath a virtuous wife, for the number of his days shall be double.''

Full appreciation of this truth may encourage men and women to make their marriages more enjoyable.

God Makes Marriages

A Roman matron asked a Jewish sage: "The Bible states that God created the world in six days. What has God been doing since that time?"

"God makes marriages," the sage replied.

"Is that all? Why, I can do that!"

She gathered a thousand of her male slaves; lined them up in single file, and placed an equal number of her female slaves opposite them. Then she declared each opposite pair married and performed thereby one thousand marriages with a single stroke!

"You see," she strutted, "I am like your God. I can make marriages."

The very next morning the matron was awakened by a great commotion. She looked out her window and saw her male and female slaves crowding her courtyard, all in an uproar, shouting and crying out: "I do not want this woman!" "I do not want this man!" Some had broken limbs. Some had black eyes. Some had torn hair. All was confusion.

The Roman matron summoned the sage, and said humbly and meekly: "You spoke the truth. Only God makes marriages."

COMMENT

This ancient legend brings into sharp focus an old Jewish doctrine that marriages are divinely ordained. How this doctrine may be defended in the modern world, with the ever-increasing tide of divorces, the author attempted to show in his book *Marriage Made in Heaven*. Briefly, his thesis is that if married folks would undertake to treat one another lovingly, in keeping with the divine Torah guidance, they would find joy and happiness and be able to bear testimony that "God makes marriages."

The Doctor's Mistake Made a Man Out of Him

A young couple living in Rio de Janeiro were always disagreeing and quarreling with one another. They were both very young, highly excitable, and unhappy. For a time, they thought that they were incompatible and that their marriage would end in divorce.

One day the woman went to her physician for an examination concerning a number of complaints. The doctor found a certain condition which he thought was cancer. He did not tell this to the woman. He called her husband and revealed his fears to him. He urged him to have his wife come in for regular periodic observation.

The news that his young wife might be suffering from a malignancy struck the husband like a thunderbolt. From that day he became a different person. He treated his wife with the greatest patience and consideration; he went out of his way to satisfy her, to bring a happy smile to her face. His motto, buried deep as a secret resolve in his heart, was, "Whatever happens tomorrow, let me not be ashamed of my actions of today."

Need it be added that this formula brought a miracle to their home? The couple grew so attached to each other that they became an example of marital happiness and bliss to all their neighbors and friends.

Fortunately, this true story has a happy ending. Within a short time the doctor realized that his diagnosis was wrong; the woman was enjoying good health.

Many years have passed since the day when the husband was so frightfully misinformed about his wife's condition, but he now thinks of that nightmare with gratitude. In its wake he underwent a spiritual metamorphosis that made him kindly, patient, forgiving, helpful, always desiring to bring cheerfulness, encouragement, and contentment into his wife's life. Moreover, it also brought *him* happiness. "The doctor's error," he would sum up, "made a man out of me."

COMMENT

Oftentimes, a word, a mere word, may have a profound influence upon a person. Psychiatrists, perhaps more than others, see this at times in their private practice. This was also known by the ancients. The psalmist, in describing those smitten with grave sickness, said, "Their soul abhorred all manner of food, and they drew near unto the gates of death," but when they turned to God in prayer, "He sent His word and healed them" (Psalms 107:18–20). The correct word at the proper time and place can bring help and health.

The Baal Shem and a Sinner

The founder of Hasidism, Reb Israel ben Eliezer, generally known as Baal Shem Tov, "master of the good name," was born in Okup, Ukraine, about 1700. His title refers to a mishnaic aphorism: "There are three crowns: the crown of learning, the crown of priesthood, and the crown of royalty, but the crown of a good name excels them all" (Ethics of the Fathers 4:17).

It happened once that a young Jewish woman left her husband and children without notice, leaving no trace. Her family were frantic. They searched and prayed. They checked every clue and spoke to everyone. After two days they discovered that she had fallen in love with a non-Jew and had crept away, on his advice, to live in a cloister where she would receive religious instruction, be baptized, and marry her lover.

The family was heartbroken. They turned to the Baal Shem Tov for help. He was on friendly terms with the priest, who had a high regard for him, and received permission from him to visit the woman and speak to her. The woman's family could not join him, and he could talk to her only in the priest's presence.

The following words are attributed to Reb Israel Baal Shem (by Dr. J. L. Snitzer in his book *The Story of the Baal Shem*): "You needn't be frightened, daughter. I haven't come to dissuade you from doing what you have made up your mind to do. If you are fully convinced that the Christian religion is more beautiful than the Jewish, you are entitled to your choice, for in the presence of the great and mighty Creator there exists no compulsion. He has given man a free will and the right to choose his own way.

"Often, however, a person enters upon a certain road without definite convictions, but because he is the victim of passion, and he imagines that a change may help him. When an individual who is thus afflicted belongs only to himself, the situation is not so very grave. He alone will be the sufferer. He alone, after the fires of passion have died down, will be consumed by the fires of conscience. But when a person abandons children, his own flesh and blood, in order to gratify his appetites, I don't know what to call a person like that. Every wild beast, every bird of prey makes a sacrifice for the sake of its child, whilst man, who bears the image of God, has no sense of piety!

"This is all I have to say,," said Reb Israel, and then turning to the priest he added, "and I thank you for having given me permission to speak these few words."

The Baal Shem Tov rose to leave. The woman, with tears falling, jumped up and cried, "No, no, don't leave me here! Don't leave me here! I'm going with you." She understood the pain she was causing others and herself.

COMMENT

The words of Reb Israel Baal Shem Tov are true in our society no less than they were in his lifetime. Many young people forsake the moral and religious path without convictions, out of ignorance and passing passions, little realizing the havoc they bring upon those who love them most.

"Take heed lest passion sway
Thy judgment to do aught which else free will
Would not admit."

John Milton (1608–1674)
Paradise Lost, Book 8, line 635

"They who go
Feel not the pain of parting; it is they
Who stay behind that suffer."

Henry Wadsworth
Longfellow (1807–1882)
Michael Angelo

A Pit and a Weasel as Witnesses

There was a small Jewish community in ancient Assyria whose members would undertake pilgrimages to Jerusalem for one or more of the three biblically ordained pilgrimage festivals: Passover, Pentecost, and Tabernacles.

Once a young Assyrian Jew was taking such a trip to Jerusalem. When he arrived at the outskirts of an Israeli border town, he heard a cry for help. Rushing in the direction of the voice, he came to a deep pit and to his astonishment found that a young girl had fallen in and was unable to get out. Hearing the man, the girl begged his help.

"You are a messenger of God sent to rescue me," she sighed.

The young man's thoughts, however, were different. Seeing the girl completely helpless he decided to take advantage of her.

"I will help you out on one condition," was his proposal.

"What is the condition?" asked the frightened girl.

"It is that you promise to fulfill my wish when I deliver you out of this hole," he replied without qualms.

After a moment of hesitation, realizing that she would perish if left in the pit, she accepted his condition.

The young man lay down on the ground beside the pit, stretched out his hand, took hold of the girl's hand, and helped her crawl out to safety. Then he demanded that she keep her promise and allow him to be intimate with her.

The young maiden was as wise as she was fair. She used her wisdom eloquently to dissuade him from this act.

"You saved my life and have performed one of the noblest human acts. As for me, in thankfulness for what you did, I belong to you. You are free to do with me as you please. However, why should you do something shameful? I will speak to my parents and tell them what you did for me. I am certain that they will not withhold me from you. We can be married, and I'll be yours for life."

The man was persuaded. He took her name and address and swore that he would return in due time to marry her as she had suggested. She, too, swore that she would wait for him.

"But who will witness our oaths?" the young man asked.

At that moment a weasel ran by.

"Let the pit and the weasel be our witnesses," the girl replied.

"Agreed," the man affirmed.

They parted. He continued on his journey to Jerusalem and she returning to her parents' home. She understood that he would come for her after he had visited Jerusalem and returned to his hometown to obtain his parents' blessings for their marriage.

When the man returned to his home in Assyria, even before he had a chance to tell his adventures to his parents, he was introduced to a beautiful young lady with whom he fell in love, and forgetting his oath, he married her. Within two years, two children were born to them.

Shortly thereafter two calamities fell upon the family in quick succession. One day a friend was carrying the older child, and as she passed by a dry cistern, suddenly the child jumped from her arms, fell into the pit, and was killed. The parents were heartbroken. The mother sought consolation from her young infant, whom she guarded now very carefully.

Nevertheless, the very next day, as she was carrying the child, a wild weasel jumped out of nowhere and, grasping the child by its arm, dashed its skull against a nearby rock. Before anything could be done, the child was dead.

The parents were overcome with grief and could not be consoled, especially the mother. When the shock subsided in some measure, she said to her husband: "Both of our children have died unnaturally. There must be a reason for it. Think hard. Tell me what you have done to cause us to deserve this punishment."

At this the husband recalled the oath he had given to the girl whose life he had saved and how he had accepted the pit and the weasel as witnesses to the oath.

"How stupid of you to violate a solemn oath," his wife reprimanded him. "So the two witnesses you set up, the pit and the weasel, have come to administer judgment upon us. I now see that you do not belong to me. You belong to the other woman. I cannot live with you any longer."

Several months after the couple was divorced, the man set out to look for the young lady he had so deceitfully forsaken. When he arrived in her hometown, however, he learned that she was mentally ill. Nevertheless, this time he was determined to do all he could to fulfill his oath. He went to her parents and asked permission to see her and to speak to her.

"For what reason?" the parents inquired.

"I hope to ask for her hand in marriage," the man replied.

The heartbroken parents were surprised and told him of their daughter's tragedy. For a year or more she had wonderful prospects of marriage. Young, admirable men sought her hand in marriage. She refused them all for no good reason, mumbling to herself words that sounded like "pit" and "weasel." They tried to reason with her, to persuade her, without success. For the last year or so, her mind seemed to wander and she had no hold on reality. "For this reason, we cannot see that any purpose could be served in your seeing our daughter," the grieving parents concluded.

The young man persisted in his request and finally was permitted to see her. He found her lying in bed, her hair disheveled, mumbling words that were hardly audible. As he listened he could discern the words "pit" and "weasel." He called her by name and started talking: "I am the man who swore to marry you, and you swore to wait for me. You suggested the pit and the weasel as the witnesses to our oath. You kept your oath faithfully. I am here now to fulfill my oath to you, if you will have me."

As he kept repeating these sentences slowly, clearly, with feeling, a change came over the woman.

A new light shone from her eyes, she sat up and smiled, she asked for a comb and brush, and then for a dress. She recognized him, she believed him, and she was rational. The parents could hardly believe the miracle. Within a short time they were married, and as all good stories end, they lived happily ever after.

COMMENT

The rabbis in the Talmud and in other ancient writings emphasized the gravity of a false oath, saying that it is an unpardonable sin. "The whole world trembled at the time when the Holy One, blessed be He, said at Sinai: 'Thou shalt not take the name of the Lord thy God in vain.' And it is of such a transgressor that the Torah says, 'the Lord will not hold him guiltless,' namely, will not leave him unpunished. And morever, for all the transgressions in the Torah, the sinner alone is punished, but in this case he and his family" (Talmud, Shevuot 39a). The truth of these statements is, of course, well demonstrated in the preceding story.

For these reasons saintly men throughout the generations have avoided swearing altogether. In fact, the laws of many civilized countries provide that people with scruples about swearing may "affirm" whenever an oath is required.

The psalmist wrote: "Lord, who shall sojourn in Thy tabernacle? Who shall dwell upon Thy holy mountain? . . . He that sweareth even to his own hurt, and changeth not" (Psalms 15:1, 4).